FROM MILITARY TO ACADEMY

T0168111

FROM MILITARY TO ACADEMY

*The Writing and Learning
Transitions of Student-Veterans*

MARK BLAAUW-HARA

UTAH STATE UNIVERSITY PRESS
Logan

© 2021 by University Press of Colorado

Published by Utah State University Press
An imprint of University Press of Colorado
245 Century Circle, Suite 202
Louisville, Colorado 80027

 ASSOCIATION of UNIVERSITY PRESSES The University Press of Colorado is a proud member of the Association of University Presses.

The University Press of Colorado is a cooperative publishing enterprise supported, in part, by Adams State University, Colorado State University, Fort Lewis College, Metropolitan State University of Denver, Regis University, University of Colorado, University of Northern Colorado, University of Wyoming, Utah State University, and Western Colorado University.

∞ This paper meets the requirements of the ANSI/NISO Z39.48–1992 (Permanence of Paper)

ISBN: 978-1-64642-133-6 (paperback)
ISBN: 978-1-64642-134-3 (ebook)
https://doi.org/10.7330/9781646421343

Library of Congress Cataloging-in-Publication Data

Names: Blaauw-Hara, Mark, author.
Title: From military to academy : the writing and learning transitions of student-veterans / by Mark Blaauw-Hara.
Description: Logan : Utah State University Press, [2021] I Includes bibliographical references and index.
Identifiers: LCCN 2021021091 (print) I LCCN 2021021092 (ebook) I ISBN 9781646421336 (paperback) I ISBN 9781646421343 (ebook)
Subjects: LCSH: Veterans—Education (Higher)—United States. I College-student veterans—United States. I English language—Rhetoric—Study and teaching (Higher) I Academic writing—Study and teaching (Higher)
Classification: LCC UB357 .B525 2021 (print) I LCC UB357 (ebook) I DDC 378.1/9826970973—dc23
LC record available at https://lccn.loc.gov/2021021091
LC ebook record available at https://lccn.loc.gov/2021021092

The University Press of Colorado gratefully acknowledges the support of North Central Michigan College toward the publication of this book.

Cover photographs: © Pankratov Yuriy/Shutterstock (top), © matabum/Shutterstock (bottom)

CONTENTS

ACKNOWLEDGMENTS

Thank you to the service members, veterans, and students who were willing to help me with this research. I literally could not have done it without you. Thank you for your service and sacrifice. I hope that this book helps to support the educational journeys of your fellow service members and student-veterans.

Thanks as well to my many academic mentors who taught me how to research, write, and think. I want to specifically note Louise Wetherbee Phelps, Kevin DePew, Michelle Navarre Cleary, and Julia Romberger, who helped me so much with the early stages of this project. Cheri Lemieux Spiegel provided an unending well of moral support. Thanks also to the vibrant community of researchers who are delving into student-veterans' writing trajectories—I relied on your work quite a bit as I developed this book. I am very grateful to North Central Michigan College for providing me sabbatical time to work on this manuscript.

An early version of chapter 1 appeared in *Composition Forum*, and an early version of chapter 2 appeared in the *Community College Journal of Research and Practice*. Both benefited from the careful reading and response of the editors and anonymous reviewers. And thank you so much to Rachael at Utah State University Press and the anonymous reviewers who read my drafts with care and provided excellent suggestions for revision.

Finally, thank you to my brilliant wife, Jami, to my sons, Joad and Harper, and to my parents and in-laws for supporting me.

FROM MILITARY TO ACADEMY

INTRODUCTION AND METHODOLOGY

Higher education is experiencing an almost unprecedented influx of student-veterans. A report from the US Department of Education found that in 2007–2008, about 657,000 veterans and 215,000 reservists or active-duty service members were undergraduates (Radford 2011). By 2013, these numbers had increased to over 1 million student-veterans; 73 percent of these students were male, and many had families (US Department of Veterans Affairs 2014). Additionally, 62 percent of them were first-generation college students, and only 15 percent were of what are thought of as traditional college ages (US Department of Veterans Affairs 2014). By 2020, over 5 million post-9/11 service members had transitioned out of the military (American Council on Education 2015), many of whom will likely use their GI Bill benefits to go to college. A 2012 American Council on Education report stated that "institutions have not faced such a significant influx of veteran students on campus since World War II" (McBain et al. 2012, 5).

In many ways, student-veterans are ideal college students. I have taught writing at a small community college with a significant student-veteran population for around twenty years, and I have found that veterans often possess strong organizational skills and a developed work ethic, among other traits. Their attendance is frequently exemplary, and they reliably do their homework. My anecdotal observations are supported by scholarship; for example, Stone (2017) notes that "military members acquired time management skills, confidence in themselves during challenging circumstances, cognitive flexibility when solving problems or evaluating information, and openness to diversity" (382). Other researchers have pointed out that student-veterans have been trained to be leaders and mutually reliant team members (Morrow and Hart 2014). They also tend to have "grit," a term popularized by Angela Duckworth to describe "having resilience in the face of failure [and] having deep commitments that you remain loyal to over many years" (qtd. in Perkins-Gough 2013, 15). In fact, one of the first studies Duckworth and her colleagues performed

DOI: 10.7330/9781646421343.c000

established that the "grittier" West Point cadets were, the more likely they were to finish their training. I have seen that same strong work ethic and ability to persevere in the face of difficult challenges carry student-veterans through draft after draft of papers.

Additionally, many student-veterans have a more developed and nuanced worldview than most traditional students, a result of working with diverse people in the military and experiencing different cultures around the world, and they can bring this experience to bear in class discussions and papers (Morrow and Hart 2014; Schell and Kleinbart 2014; Stone 2017). In a commentary in the *Chronicle of Higher Education*, Mark Street (2014) describes the enriched perspectives veterans have brought to his visual arts classes, noting that they provide a valuable counterpoint to the views of more traditional students. He writes, "Yes, let's do all we can to make the transition from military service to college classroom easier for the nation's recent veterans. But let's also remember that we're not doing it only for them, we're doing it for us" (para. 10). The American Council on Education (2011) report *Promising Practices in Veterans' Education* found that student-veterans defined success more broadly than many traditional students, including not only GPA, but also social success and engagement with faculty and their peers—a welcome finding to faculty who strive semester after semester to get students to think beyond grades.

Despite these strengths, veterans frequently find the transition to college difficult. In a *Chronicle* cover story, Libby Sander (2012) writes that military programs designed to help veterans transition to civilian life focus more on how to access healthcare and get a job than they do on choosing a college and getting educational benefits. Additionally, colleges frequently have systems that are disorienting for veterans. Rumann, Rivera, and Hernandez (2011) report that student-veterans are often "sent from office to office when attempting to gather information related to GI Bill funding" (55), and that college staff differ greatly in their knowledge about veterans' benefits. "From Soldier to Student II" found "great diversity in how institutions serve veterans, the variety of services and programs offered, and where services and programs are housed within the administrative infrastructure" (McBain et al. 2012, 8). Advising and faculty training to work with veterans tends to vary widely (Persky and Oliver 2010; Wheeler 2012), and frequently training programs for how to address veteran-specific issues are inadequate (McBain et al. 2012). Veterans are post-traditional students, and many college orientation programs are designed with more traditional students in mind. As Holly Wheeler (2012) writes, "After having served in the military, likely in overseas combat, veterans do not need to be shown around campus or to spend an entire day meeting 18-year-old classmates" (790). Wheeler suggests that colleges develop specialized orientations for veterans that are designed to help them navigate financial aid, meet other student-veterans, and introduce them to college resources. Currently, however, few colleges provide such orientations. In a meta-analysis of over sixty publications centering on student-veterans and college, Evans, Pellegrino, and Hoggan (2015) were able to find "no overarching frameworks to help administrators make decisions about appropriate support structures they can design for veterans. Even more surprising was the lack of empirical studies pertaining to the efficacy of existing institutional supports" (57).

Another problem, as Hart and Thompson (2013) have discovered, is that much training for college personnel operates on the assumption of deficits, focusing primarily on the ways student-veterans may be behind academically or the length of time they have been away from formal schooling. Despite the good intentions of the trainers, such training sessions do not recognize the diversity of the student-veteran community or the ways in which their military experiences may support college success. In addition to noting the dangers of stereotyping the veteran community (for example, not all have seen combat, and not all have PTSD), Hart and Thompson note that "most faculty report high achievement among veterans, as well as a high sense of initiative, professionalism, and leadership" (4). Similarly to Street, the faculty who participated in Hart and Thompson's study were grateful for the "varied cultural experiences and broader worldviews" veterans brought to their classes (4). Faculty frequently characterized student-veterans as "mature, serious students who seek frank, direct guidance as they develop as writers" (4). Lighthall (2012) points out that student-veterans "are emotionally mature, goal-oriented, mission-driven, experienced leaders . . . They are the kind of role models we need on our campuses" (89). Of course, as Vaccaro (2015) points out, "one size fits all" conceptions of the needs and strengths of student-veterans are not only ineffective, they are also frustrating to student-veterans themselves. Still, as I try to do in this study, it is possible to identify likely characteristics of the student-veteran population as a whole and use those characteristics to at least begin shaping productive interventions.

STUDENT-VETERANS AND COLLEGE WRITING

In addition to studies that address student-veterans' college transition in a general sense, there is a growing body of research that focuses specifically on how they experience college writing. The most complete study is one I mentioned earlier: Alexis Hart and Roger Thompson's (2013) *"An Ethical Obligation": Promising Practices for Student-Veterans in College Writing Classrooms.* The study is the result of a 2011 CCCC research grant and represents growing interest in student-veterans from the college writing community. Hart and Thompson's two-year study involved surveys, site visits, and interviews with faculty, staff, students, administrators, and veteran support personnel at over fifty colleges. The other major piece of recent scholarship is *Generation Vet: Composition, Student-Veterans, and the Post-9/11 University.* This collection of essays, edited by Sue Doe and Lisa Langstraat (2014), features chapters by some of the foremost writers on student-veterans and academic writing. Taken together, they provide wide-ranging multiple perspectives on veterans' transition to the academy that are profoundly useful to writing faculty. Additionally, several journals, such as *Composition Forum,* have released special issues focused on veterans' experiences, and veteran-focused articles have appeared in *Teaching English in the Two-Year College, College Composition and Communication,* and a number of other journals. Importantly, the *Journal of Veterans Studies* was formed in 2016, representing a publication venue for cross-disciplinary research on veterans' experiences.

This growing body of research has served to enrich the portrayal of student-veterans. For example, it likely comes as a surprise to many faculty that enlisted military service people tend to write quite a lot, especially if they have been promoted into supervisory roles. As Hinton (2013) points out, their military writing experience means that student-veterans should not be viewed as novice writers, even though they are new to college writing. In fact, they often have a very accomplished sense of audience and purpose, and they understand the military genres in which they have written quite well. Many media portrayals paint enlisted service as primarily consisting of firing weapons and following orders; however, an examination of training materials for enlisted troops and military educational theory (which I address in detail in chapter 2) shows that service members at all levels are encouraged to think critically and solve problems, most frequently in teams. As Doe and Doe (2013) point out, all branches of the military put a heavy emphasis on training and learning, since they need to transform recruits from all walks of life and levels of prior knowledge into sailors, soldiers, airmen, or marines. This training and learning takes many forms, including those many faculty would recognize, such as book discussions and case-study analyses. Additionally, as I noted above, the military trains its members to develop responsibility, self-efficacy, grit, and other qualities that support success in college.

In short, student-veterans are a complex group. It is true that most of them have been away from traditional schooling for a period of years, and they will likely be rusty at "student-ing" practices such as sitting in a classroom, taking notes, and reading textbooks. Also, some may have joined the military, at least in part, because they did not enjoy formal K-12 schooling and wanted a break, or because they may not have considered themselves "college material" at age eighteen. As I noted earlier, many of them struggle with accessing their veteran benefits, deciding on an academic path, dealing with possible PTSD and the psychological aftereffects of war, and discerning how to reintegrate into civilian society. However, in many ways, student-veterans are better prepared to succeed in college than some of their civilian peers. We can help them build on these strengths by better understanding the military and how it functions as a learning organization, and by better understanding the types of writing and learning student-veterans did while they were in the military. It is true that many entering student-veterans do not know a lot about college; however, it is also true that we do not know a lot about them.

My primary goal in this book is to help colleges—and especially writing faculty—better understand student-veterans so they can smooth the transition from the military to the academy. I hope to fill some of the knowledge gaps many faculty hold about the writing and learning experiences of student-veterans while they were in the military, and to provide a detailed picture of how student-veterans may experience the transition to college and academic writing. In this book, I provide an overview of how theories of community membership and identity construction provide context for understanding how service members see themselves in the military and college, drawing from scholarship on communities of practice, threshold concepts, student retention and success, and more. I also supply specific suggestions for writing faculty to help student-veterans recognize and build on the strengths they have developed during their military service.

RESEARCH SITE

North Central Michigan College (NCMC) is a small community college located near the tip of Michigan's Lower Peninsula. It enrolls between 2,500–3,000 students, of whom around 100 have self-identified as military veterans. The college's annual budget hovers near $15 million, and it employs around 100 full-time faculty, staff, and administrators as well as about 200 part-time staff and adjunct faculty. NCMC has three primary campuses: one in Petoskey, considered its main campus, which offers all programs and courses, and two in nearby cities that offer limited courses. It also offers a small number of courses at other locations. Around half of NCMC's students usually declare the intent to earn occupational degrees; the other half expect to transfer to a university or pursue liberal arts degrees.

While its size and budget make it difficult for the college to provide the same level of infrastructure for student-veterans as do some larger schools, NCMC's efforts to support its student-veterans have earned it distinction as a "military friendly" college for much of the past decade (Military Friendly 2018). The college has a dedicated student-veteran advisor, and NCMC also connects student-veterans with other veteran services in the area, such as employment representatives and county veteran service officers.

The college also has an active chapter of the Student Veterans of America (SVA), although its numbers tend to be small. NCMC holds regular programs that show its support of veterans, such as featuring speeches by Derek Blumke, the co-founder of SVA and an alumnus of NCMC, and Dakota Meyer, a Medal of Honor recipient. The college also hosts an annual Veterans' Day breakfast that is attended by community veterans and their families. And, like most colleges, NCMC employs staff and faculty who are veterans themselves.

I worked at NCMC for two decades. My status as a faculty member and writing program administrator (WPA) provided me with experience and access that helped gather data for this study; additionally, it highlighted the need to maintain robust anonymity and confidentiality protocols. As I detail in my sections on participant selection and data collection, these protocols were necessary to ensure not just valid data, but willing and comfortable participants. Many of the veterans I interviewed were current students at the college (although, with the exception of the informal pilot interview group, they were not students in my classes). Without appropriate confidentiality provisions, they might worry that what they said would get back to their instructors and perhaps cause problems for them. As I explained to my participants, I kept all data filed and printed by pseudonym, and the document that linked pseudonyms to real names was kept in a password-encrypted file.

METHODOLOGY AND STUDY PARTICIPANTS

Because of the relatively unexplored nature of this area of study, I adopted a qualitative approach. As Creswell (2012) writes, qualitative research is best suited to situations when "the literature might yield little information about the phenomenon of study, and you need to learn more from participants through exploration" (16). The research is open-ended and guided, in large part, by what is learned from the participants. Stake (1995) writes that a key characteristic of qualitative research is that its central goal is to understand what is happening rather than to predict or explain (37). These descriptions characterize my goals in my own research: to explore a relatively new area, to learn from my participants, and to understand their experience.

I centered my research on a series of veteran case studies. Robert Yin (2009) writes that "the distinctive need for case studies arises out of the desire to understand complex social phenomena. In brief, the case study method allows investigators to retain the holistic and meaningful characteristics of real-life events" (4). Yin's discussion of multiple-case design, wherein the researcher studies several similar cases, is of particular application to my research goals. Single-case studies are vulnerable to allegations that the case is unique; while the goal of case-study research is not necessarily to generalize the findings, studying multiple cases allows the researcher to look for trends across the cases and offset potential criticism that the cases are unique (60–62). Since I hoped to identify such trends, I decided to study multiple student-veterans.

The specific description for the type of case studies I did is "collective instrumental case studies," which is drawn from Robert Stake. Stake (1995) defines an instrumental case study as one that provides insight into an issue, as opposed to an intrinsic case study where the goal is to understand the particular case (3). Collective instrumental case studies, then, are "instrumental stud[ies] extended to several cases . . . They are chosen because it is believed that understanding them will lead to better understanding, perhaps better theorizing, about a still larger collection of cases" (Stake 1998, 89). In Stake's (1995) description of issues that are appropriate for this type of research, he writes that they "are not simple and clean, but intricately wired to political, social, historical, and especially personal contexts" (17). This certainly describes veterans' transition to college writing. It is my hope that my case studies of student-veterans will lead to a better understanding of the transitions to academic writing that are experienced by the "larger collection of cases" of student-veterans as a whole—or at least provide the first steps in that direction.

For my analysis of the case studies, I chose to adapt a constructivist grounded-theory methodology most clearly articulated by Kathy Charmaz (2006), who emphasizes flexibility and interaction, highlighting the co-construction of theory through the interplay between participants' words and views and the researcher's interpretation (9–10). Creswell (2012) notes that grounded theorists remain open to developing their research methodology as they progress through the study, always remaining responsive to their data (which they code as they go) and their participants (431–432). Grounded theorists continue to gather data until they make the subjective determination that they have reached "saturation," a point where "new data will not provide any new information or insights for the developing categories" (433). Frequently, this means that grounded theorists have fewer participants than might be expected, since they continue only until they see clear patterns.

As I developed my methodology, I looked to a number of earlier studies for models of successful case-study research involving small numbers of participants. I found a well-established track record in writing studies of such qualitative research. The most significant to me was Roz Ivanič's (1998) *Writing and Identity: The Discoursal Construction of Identity in Academic Writing*, which was based on case studies of eight adult post-traditional students who were over twenty-five, native speakers of English, and "had experienced some sort of difficulty with academic writing" (111). Ivanič found her participants either through mutual contacts or because she had been their writing tutor. Ivanič analyzed one academic essay from each participant and interviewed them about the choices they made in writing the essay, as well as conducting another interview about participants' literacy histories and current practices. She also integrated her observations of her participants and tried to interview their writing tutors; however, the amount of interaction she had with each participant varied, and she was unable to interview all of the tutors. Ivanič argues that this methodology allowed her to "make generalizations about the nature of writer identity," but that the study was too small to generalize about how student characteristics (such as race or whether they came from a working-class background) might affect the difficulties each student had (113). Despite her small sample size, Ivanič's book is a significant contribution to the field, widely cited in research on academic discourse and student identity.

As I continued to read in preparation for this project, I encountered a number of other researchers who had used case-study research as a method to examine discourse, academic literacy, transitions to college, and other areas that pertained to my research. For example, Christine Pearson Casanave (2002) conducted case studies for *Writing Games*, her book on academic writing and identity. Casanave relied mainly on open interviews in which she had a set of prepared questions, but she used the questions as a starting point and let the conversation develop naturally:

I was never absolutely sure where one of these conversations would lead . . . I was mainly interested in listening to what people had to say about themselves, about their writing and their writing practices and attitudes, and in watching them discover things about themselves as writers along the way . . . I want to interact with, analyze, and depict real people, not cases, and to impart an embodied sense of their selves in the stories I construct. (32–33)

The human-centered methodology Ivanič and Casanave used appealed to me, as my goals also were to portray the experiences of a small number of participants as individuals and then attempt to draw conclusions from those experiences. Other researchers I encountered further demonstrated the flexibility of the case-study approach and its ability to simultaneously present participants as multifaceted individuals while allowing researchers to make limited generalizations (e.g., Herrington and Curtis 2000; Hinton 2013; Popken 1996; Prior 1998; Rumann and Hamrick 2010). Data collection varied among these studies: single or multiple interviews, observation notes, examination of pieces of writing, participant self-reflections, and so on. In sum, case-study research is used in the field as a flexible, reliable methodology that can generate solid data, especially if the area under study is relatively new.

For my formal study, over the course of 2014–2016 I recruited nine student-veterans who agreed to tell me about their experiences writing and learning in the military and college. I used a combination of snowball sampling (in which participants suggested other possible participants drawn from their social networks) and volunteer sampling, in which I asked writing instructors, my school's veterans' academic advisor, and the local chapter of Student Veterans of America to share a call for study volunteers. Admittedly, these methods do not produce a statistically random sampling, and so this study should be viewed as exploratory. However, as the participant list demonstrates, I was able to interview a mix of male and female students who were veterans of all service branches. The pseudonyms, service histories, and brief descriptions of my participants follow. The ages listed, as well as their progress toward their degrees, were at the time of their interviews.

- Brian is a twenty-seven-year-old male army veteran. He enlisted at age nineteen and served for seven and a half years. When he left the service, his rank was SGT (E5)—sergeant, E5 pay grade. He is an advanced college undergraduate.
- Amy is a twenty-six-year-old female marine veteran. She enlisted after a year of college at age nineteen and served for five years, leaving with a rank of SGT (E5). She is close to graduation.

- John is a twenty-eight-year-old male marine veteran. He enlisted at age eighteen and served for eight years, leaving as a SGT (E5). He is about a year into his undergraduate degree.

- Logan is a thirty-one-year-old male navy veteran. He enlisted at age eighteen and served for ten and a half years, leaving with a rank of STG1(SW) (E6)—sonar technician first class, surface warfare specialist, E6 pay grade. For the past two years, he has served in the army national guard and is currently a calvary scout, SGT (E5). He is an advanced college undergraduate.

- Joseph is a thirty-two-year-old male army veteran. He enlisted at age twenty-one and is still serving. Currently, he is in the army reserve, holding the rank of SGT (E5) with a military occupational specialty of 46Q (public affairs specialist). He has a BA in English with an emphasis in journalism.

- Ryanne is a thirty-three-year-old female navy veteran. She enlisted at age seventeen and served for four years. When she left, her rank was 2nd class petty officer (E5). She is about midway through her associate's degree.

- Derek is a thirty-three-year-old male air force veteran. He enlisted at age eighteen and served for six years as an aircraft mechanic. He left active duty with the rank of SSGT (E5) and subsequently served in the Air National Guard for six years, leaving with a rank of TSGT (E6). He holds a bachelor's degree in psychology and political science.

- Mike is a forty-five-year-old male veteran of the army and coast guard. He enlisted in the army at age seventeen when he was a senior in high school and served for four years as an MP (E4). After a brief stint as a civilian, he enlisted in the coast guard at twenty-one and served for twenty-four years, ultimately retiring with a rank of E6. This is his first semester of college.

- Alan is a twenty-five-year-old male army veteran. He enlisted at age seventeen and served for nearly 6 years. When he left the army, his rank was SGT (E5) in the infantry. He is close to his associate's degree.

I provided each of these veterans with a consent form and a short survey before the interview, both of which appear in appendix A. Although my supervising institution's institutional review board (IRB) agreed that a consent form was not strictly necessary for my research, I thought it was best to give my participants as full an understanding of the process as possible. After asking demographic and background questions, I transitioned to open-ended questions in which I tried not to constrain their responses. For example, one of my questions asked how my participants' military experience shaped their sense of identity. Another asked why they had decided to go to college and whether they had any concerns about the likelihood of their success.

My interviews were semi-structured and informal, and I focused on "the establishment of a human-to-human relation with the respondent and the desire to understand rather than to explain" (Fontana and Frey 1998, 56–57). Blakeslee and Fleischer (2010) write that informal interviews are more flexible than formal interviews, allowing the researcher to shape the interview in response to the conversation with the participant (132–133). As can be seen in appendix A, I generated a short list of primary and follow-up questions for my interviews; however, I stressed to my participants that I was very interested in hearing what they had to say, and that they were free to deviate from the questions if they wished. I also asked follow-up questions that were directly related to what the individual veterans shared in their interviews, making each interview a unique experience. Charmaz (2006) suggests that interviewers "devise a few broad, open-ended questions. Then you can focus your interview questions to invite detailed discussion of the topic" (26). This is what I attempted to do.

Stake (1998) suggests that the researcher avoid taking copious notes during the interview, instead focusing on listening and asking clarifying questions. Accordingly, I took minimal notes, instead electing to digitally record each interview and have them transcribed. Stake (1998) also recommends that the researcher plan time immediately after the interview to write detailed notes, paying special attention to what might not come through in the transcript (such as context and innuendo). I followed this advice, writing research memos to myself immediately after each interview and at many stages in the coding and writing process.

DATA ANALYSIS

I analyzed my data consistently with grounded-theory protocols laid out by Kathy Charmaz (2006). The first step was to code the interview transcripts and surveys for key themes. For the first run—initial coding—Charmaz recommends that the researcher quickly move through the data while remaining open to "all possible theoretical directions indicated by your readings of the data" (46). These initial codes are provisional and can be used to show where there is a need for more data as well as representing the data one already has. I generated a great many initial codes as I read through the interview transcripts. Some examples from Brian's interview are in table 0.1, with my initial codes in the left-hand column.

After developing initial codes, I moved to focused coding, where I identified themes between codes. As Blakeslee and Fleischer (2010)

Table 0.1. Initial interview coding

Pursuing what needs to be done	Brian: I think the biggest thing, the biggest aspect, I learned in the army is to aggressively pursue what needs to be done. So if I had an issue or trouble with something, I would be able to seek out how to fix it or how to figure out how to do it. So whether it's by finding it myself or finding someone who knows how I would need to write something better or find information on something I need to write about. That's what I would say I drew from the military: I could, like, buckle down and get it done.
Feeling embarrassed to be older	Brian: You don't feel, like, ashamed, but you're just kind of embarrassed to be going to school with kids. Twenty-seven years old, and it's, some of them are high-schoolers, seventeen- and eighteen-year-olds that are seniors in high school that are doing good in high school so they get [the school experience], which is great, you know, great deal for them. And it's kind of a little bit hard to relate.

write, the process of looking for themes in interview transcripts can be somewhat circular and involves reading first to discern patterns and themes, and then reading again (and, perhaps, again and again) to see how strong and significant the patterns are (175). For this stage of analysis, I reread my initial codes and transcripts/surveys, looking for which initial codes were most prevalent and seemed to best explain the data. I also looked for instances where I had coded essentially the same thing using different terms and decided which was the best term to use, and I looked through earlier data to see if I could apply some of the codes I had developed later in the process. This was a recursive and time-intensive process, but it resulted in a tight list of codes that I was confident represented my data.

For example, Brian was not the only veteran who said that the military trained him to work hard. In my focused coding, I developed a category called "transitioning to college—strengths," with a subcategory of "pursuing the mission, learning to learn." I then went back through the transcripts and surveys and highlighted in yellow statements that fit this code, which allowed me to group statements such as these together:

> DEREK: There's no way I would have gone to school [had it not been for my time in the air force]. The military taught me how to study, how to work hard, discipline, all the things that my dad wanted for me.

> JOSEPH: You're really required to always finish the mission. I mean, that's not only, it's not only an idea—in the army it's one of our warrior ethoses: "I will put the mission first." And when you translate that into the academic world or, say, a degree, if you can use those skills of putting the mission first in academics, it definitely helps you to get your job done, to think of things like deadlines or turn-in dates or upcoming exams as objectives.

MIKE: I wasn't a good student in high school at all. And I didn't have the skills to learn how to learn, so I really didn't learn how to learn until I went into the military. And in the coast guard there's a lot of written tests and a lot of studying and hitting the books. So that's really where I learned how to learn. If I went to college after high school, I would have just wasted my time and money. I wasn't disciplined enough.

After I developed my codes, I asked a colleague to read my transcripts and surveys and compare them against my codes. I asked her to evaluate whether my codes seemed true to the data and whether I had missed any significant trends. She agreed that my coding was valid, and pointed to some additional places where my participants had talked about transferring their military writing knowledge to college that I had missed.

I also wrote copious research memos. As Glesne and Peshkin (1992) suggest, writing memos to oneself as research progresses can not only record impressions from an interview, it can help the researcher develop his thoughts and spur new perspectives (128). Blakeslee and Fleischer (2010) echo this understanding, writing that research memos function not only as spaces for the researcher to reflect on the immediate interview or recent findings, but also as opportunities to speculate, to fine-tune research goals and, as the researcher rereads older memos, to uncover patterns that might have gone unnoticed (184). Accordingly, I wrote research memos after each interview, as well as at key stages of the process (distributing surveys, recruiting participants, different stages of coding) to document the process, record what I was thinking at the time, remind myself to research certain areas more, and speculate.

Some of what I discovered through the coding process—such as that student-veterans have a difficult time connecting with civilian peers—was expected. However, even expected results often contained surprising elements. For example, I did not expect age-related embarrassment to show up so strongly as a sub-element of the difficulty connecting with peers. Nor did I anticipate that another key perception veterans would have of civilian peers is that they are unreliable, or that this perception would contribute to a resistance toward collaborative activities such as study groups.

Perhaps the most surprising thing I found was how much the veterans understood about writing from their experience in the military. Probably like many college faculty, I had held a view that because much of the writing enlisted service members do in the military is short and formulaic, the service members would approach it uncritically and somewhat automatically—to use Brian's parlance, "just hand-jam it out." However, I found that the student-veterans with whom I spoke tended to have a sophisticated understanding of audience, purpose, and genre. Again drawing from Brian:

> INTERVIEWER: How would you figure out what the guy up above you was looking for [in a counseling report]?
>
> BRIAN: He would let you know. Or, I mean, you would get a vibe. The military is kind of a subculture of its own. You kind of learn how to communicate without necessarily passing the words or whatever like that, you know what I mean? You learn how to read what they're going to . . . Some NCOs, they call them, noncommissioned officers or sergeants, they'll lay it out for you step for step, "This is what I want from you." Others won't.
>
> Basically, some NCOs, they wouldn't care. They'd just hand-jam it out and get it done. But the idea behind it is to inform the soldier, to go over their career and what they were doing and what they needed to work on. So you would outline . . . that's how you want to take a soldier, say, "This is what I see of you. This is what happened. This is what we need to work on. And this is what will help your career in the army." So the idea behind it is to create success in the soldiers. That's the whole idea of the counseling statements.

I will explore my results in much greater detail in subsequent chapters. However, it may be helpful to present the major codes I settled on in table 0.2.

This methodology yielded rich data on student-veterans' transitions to the college writing and learning environment. As subsequent chapters show, the study enriches the perception of what types of writing enlisted veterans did in the military, as well as their individual understanding of genre and audience. It also reveals the ways they experience college writing and college in general, including struggles and successes. Additionally, it sheds light on how the military functions as a learning community and how it shapes the identities of service members. When possible, I connect the experiences of my participants to other scholarship, and in later chapters, I build on this data to make concrete suggestions for writing teachers and programs.

Because it is limited by its small numbers of participants and by its being conducted at a single research site, this study should not be seen as representative of all student-veterans, and one would be wise not to overgeneralize based on my findings. However, the perspectives and suggestions I present here are nonetheless valuable, and there is ample precedent in writing studies for this sort of qualitative case-study research that involves a relatively limited number of participants. For example, such research has yielded intriguing results that have advanced the field's understanding of writers' identity (Casanave

Table 0.2. Final themes and sub-themes

Enlisting, writing, and learning in the military	Enlisting out of high school, enlistment reasons Writing in the military: logs, counseling reports, reading officer expectations, learning genre conventions Learning in the military: training, tests, reading manuals
Challenges transitioning to college	Feeling like experience wasn't recognized Not fitting into traditional placement, first-year experience (FYE), developmental writing Making up for lost time between high school and college Feeling embarrassed to be going to school with "kids" Experiencing social isolation/disconnection from nonmilitary peers
Applying strengths to college	Applying work ethic, pursuing the mission Connecting with veteran community Understanding diverse people, applying life experience

2002; Ivanič 1998; Prior 1998) and students' transition to college and academic discourse (Herrington and Curtis 2000; Hinton 2013, 2014; Rumann and Hamrick 2010).

A NOTE ON GENDER AND RACE

Although I attempted to recruit more women veterans, I was able to find only two who were willing to participate. Partially, this is reflective of the demographics of the military: in 2019, women made up only 10 percent of the veteran population, although that number is expected to grow (Dever 2019). However, because of the small number of women in my study, I was unable to make any generalizations about gender differences. This is, however, a growing area of research. For example, Heineman (2017) describes ways community colleges can help support women veterans in their transitions to school, and Diramio et al. (2015) explore gender differences in how (and when) student-veterans ask for help in college. Albright et al. (2019) address women veterans' access of health services at colleges, finding a need to provide veteran outreach that differs from colleges' usual methods of outreach to female students. The American Society of Higher Education also notes differences between female and male student-veterans (ASHE 2011b). In my study, I asked both of my women participants if they felt as though their gender played a role in their military experience or their transition to college. Both noted that they felt quite comfortable as women in the military and that they did not see gender as relevant in their college transition. However, research has made it clear that this is not always the case (e.g., Baechtold and De Sawal 2009; Cheney et al. 2013; Huynh-Hohnbaum et al. 2003; Trobaugh 2018).

Race was also an unexplored area in my study. According to the most recent US Census, 92.4 percent of the residents of Emmet County—where NCMC is located—identify as white (US Census, n.d.). The next-highest ethnic group, at 3.8 percent, is American Indian and Alaskan Native. The NCMC student body has similar racial characteristics, and I felt it would be quite difficult to explore issues of race at this research site. I did not ask my participants to disclose their racial identity, and none of them discussed racial issues in their interviews. Other scholarship has explored how race impacts student-veterans' experiences with higher education (Bryan and Bryan 2015; Elliott 2014; Jenner 2017); however, like the question of gender, the impact race has on student-veterans' experiences in higher education is an emerging area of research and merits more study.

THIS BOOK'S ORGANIZATION

Chapters 1–4 present and analyze my findings from four different perspectives. They are designed to be able to be read nonsequentially, and the reader will get a better understanding of different aspects of student-veterans' transitions from each chapter. I integrate relevant scholarship throughout each chapter, and I end each with several actionable suggestions. However, the best understanding of student-veterans' transitions will be gained from treating each of these chapters as ways to focus a larger subject into manageable chunks; reading them all will give the most complete perspective.

In chapter 1, I focus on the learning communities of the military and college, with my primary theoretical lenses being communities of practice and andragogy. As Hinton (2013) and Hadlock (2012) argue, while student-veterans may be new to academic writing, they are not novice writers. Nor are they unskilled learners. Training and learning are at the heart of the military. In many ways, the learning environment of the military is significantly different from that of college—for example, it is highly community-oriented, with much of the training taking place in groups whose members are explicitly encouraged to support one another's learning. However, the modern military also shares many goals with college, including prioritizing the development of critical thinking and decision-making skills.

In chapter 2, I focus on key dispositional strengths student-veterans bring with them from the military. As I noted earlier, Hart and Thompson (2013) argue that many colleges approach student-veterans from a perspective assuming deficits, focusing on what such students lack rather than what they bring to college. In part to remedy this assumption, I connect student-veteran strengths to research on student success, persistence, and retention. I argue that although many veterans have a difficult transition to higher education, colleges can build on these strengths to help student-veterans succeed in college.

In chapter 3, I explore a common type of military writing with which student-veterans are most familiar: evaluations, or counseling reports. Every service member is evaluated by his or her superior officer several times during service, and these evaluations are regarded within the military as very important in helping individuals grow into better embodiments of the ideals within their service branches. I present evaluation forms and guidelines for writing them drawn from the US Marines, US Air Force, US Navy, and US Army, and I analyze the writing the forms require. I also present interview data from my student-veteran participants and introduce survey data from writing faculty.

Chapter 4 adopts a threshold concept lens to view student-veterans' experiences with college writing in particular. The focus here is on writing and writing classrooms, and readers who want immediate suggestions for how to make writing classes more "veteran-friendly" (Hart and Thompson 2016) could gain ideas from chapters 3 and 4 they could put into practice next week. (Of course, I think a much more complete understanding can be acquired by reading the whole book, but my point here is that it need not be read in order.) Threshold concepts, most clearly articulated by Meyer and Land (2005), represent key (albeit challenging) ideas within a discipline that students must understand if they are to move forward in that discipline. In writing studies, Adler-Kassner and Wardle's (2015) *Naming What We Know* most fully explores the field's current understanding of threshold concepts, and I identify several concepts from their book that I think connect most strongly to student-veterans. As in the previous chapters, I also provide suggestions for how faculty can use these threshold concepts to support student-veterans in writing classes.

Finally, in chapter 5, I provide overarching suggestions that draw from my case studies and scholarship presented in chapters 1–4. These suggestions are meant to coalesce the findings from the preceding chapters into a manageable list of big takeaways. Most of these focus on the writing classroom, but since the writing classroom is a smaller habitat within the larger ecosystem of the college, several suggestions also address changes to colleges on the macro level.

1
COMMUNITY AND IDENTITY

A key finding in the growing body of student-veteran research is that the subjects had a richer experience writing in the military than many college faculty assume (Hadlock 2012; Hadlock and Doe 2014; Hinton 2013, 2014; Mallory and Downs 2014). However, their ability to fluidly transfer their writing skills to the classroom is complicated by the fact that the writing they did in the military was highly situated: it was bound up in the larger practices and environment of the armed forces. Lave and Wenger (1991) have noted that situated knowledge tends to be difficult to transfer between contexts, and as I and others (e.g., Hadlock 2012; Hinton 2013) have found, many student-veterans do not conceive of themselves as writers because they do not see the connection between the highly situated writing they did in the military and that which they are being asked to do in college. They understand, for example, how to write an effective counseling report, but they may have trouble transferring the skills of clarity, directness, and evidence to academic writing.

In this chapter, I provide an overview of veterans' experiences learning and writing in the military, from the ways the armed forces seek to form a community with common purposes to how they build the competence of their service members through training (often done in teams). I then contrast the learning environment of the military to that of college, highlighting both areas of convergence, where military experience may support student-veterans' transition, and areas of disconnect that may contribute to feelings of frustration and possible disorientation (or "learning shock," a term I explore in more detail later in this chapter). Finally, I provide suggestions for how we in the academy—and specifically those of us involved with writing studies—can help student-veterans connect the two learning environments and, hopefully, increase these students' chances of success at college.

DOI: 10.7330/9781646421343.c001

LEARNING IN THE MILITARY: THEORETICAL FRAMES

Lave and Wenger's (1991) concept of communities of practice (CoPs) provides one useful theoretical frame to help understand the military as a learning environment. According to their formulation, a CoP is a group of individuals who engage in common practices, and these practices define the group. (For examples, midwives practice midwifery.) These groups contain practitioners who are at different stages of mastery of the practices, which correspond to different identities. For example, new members often fall into the apprentice role, learning the practices of the community from more experienced members, who correspond to journeymen or master practitioners. Gradually, as the apprentices gain skill and knowledge, they move toward full participation, eventually becoming masters themselves and instructing newer members.

Lave and Wenger (1991) write that "learning viewed as a situated activity has as its central defining characteristic a process that we call *legitimate peripheral participation* . . . Learners inevitably participate in communities of practitioners and . . . the mastery of knowledge and skill requires newcomers to move toward full participation in the sociocultural practices of a community" (29; my emphasis). "Legitimacy" denotes belonging in a CoP not as a transient or a dabbler but as a contributing member. "Peripheral" indicates that the member is not a "full participant" (36)—a master—but it does not equate to "lesser." Lave and Wenger characterize peripherality as positive: "[It] suggests an opening, a way of gaining access to sources for understanding through growing involvement" (37). Peripheral participants do not perform the full range of practices in the community, and they are not accorded the same level of responsibility or respect as full participants. However, their participation is welcomed and encouraged.

This final sub-concept—participation—bears more examination, especially as it relates to student-veterans. Crucially, this participation must not merely entail a reenactment of the community's practices; instead, it represents an actual contribution to the community. In Lave and Wenger's book, the apprentice midwives they use as examples are actually helping babies to be born, not just going through simulations. While more experienced members of the CoP help the newer members learn and perform the practices, new entrants to a community do not just observe the more experienced members: legitimate peripherality "crucially involves *participation* as a way of learning—of both absorbing and being absorbed in—the 'culture of practice.' An extended period of legitimate peripherality provides learners with opportunities to make the culture of practice theirs" (1991, 95).

In the military, legitimate peripherality is clear: new recruits go through a highly codified basic training program in which they learn key principles of the military community and their specific branch of the service; as they continue their service and progress up the ranks, performing more complex tasks and supervising others, they learn more about the profession and become more crucial participants. Military writing serves as a microcosm of the larger military CoP and follows a similar pattern. New participants write little, often only log entries and similar short, highly structured artifacts. As enlisted men and women are promoted, their writing expands, now including evaluations of subordinates, incident reports, memos, and the like. Officers write still more. Most of the writing has a specific format, which, as Hadlock (2012) notes, serves to make it quickly and easily understood by other members of the military community. All formal military writing—regardless of whether it is a log entry produced by a seaman, a counseling report produced by a sergeant, or a memorandum produced by an officer—is an important contribution to the military enterprise. It is not an exercise.

In addition to communities of practice, another theoretical framework that informs the military's educational and training practices is adult learning theory, or andragogy, which relies heavily on the work of Malcolm Knowles. Knowles, Holton, and Swanson (2011) write that "adults have a self-concept of being responsible for their own decisions, for their own lives. Once they have arrived at that self-concept, they develop a deep psychological need to be seen by others and treated by others as being capable of self-direction" (65). Student-veterans, especially those who have served in combat situations, have certainly become accustomed to being responsible for their decisions and are well aware of the repercussions of those decisions, yet much of traditional education is set up to serve much younger students who are less capable of self-direction. Although student-veterans are educational novices, they do not see themselves as similar to traditional-age students, and they frequently are frustrated to be grouped with them. The work of Knowles and others provides possibilities for addressing some of the strengths and challenges common to student-veterans.

In their argument for greater focus on adult learning theory, Knowles, Holton, and Swanson (2011) point out that

> all the great teachers of ancient times [such as Confucius, Lao Tse, Jesus, Aristotle, Socrates, Plato, Cicero, Evelid, and Quintilian] . . . were teachers of adults, not of children. Because their experiences were with adults, they developed a very different concept of the learning/teaching process from the one that later dominated formal education. These notable teachers

perceived learning to be a process of mental inquiry, not passive reception of transmitted content. Accordingly, they invented techniques for engaging learners in inquiry. (35)

Knowles and colleagues (2011) note that adults are more self-directed and assume more responsibility for their own lives than do children. They also have a stronger sense of personal identity. Knowles and his coauthors argue that an educational system that does not recognize these differences runs the risk not only of being ineffective, but of alienating adult learners. They lay out the following six principles of andragogy:

1. "The need to know." Adults are unlikely to take the teacher's word that a concept is important; in contrast, if they understand why they need to learn something and buy into that need, "they will invest considerable energy in probing into the benefits they will gain from learning it and the negative consequences of not learning it" (64). The authors recommend that teachers incorporate "real or simulated experiences in which the learners discover for themselves the gaps between where they are now and where they want to be" (65).

2. "The learners' self-concept." As I noted above, adults are used to self-direction. Knowles and his coauthors point out that a curriculum that removes that self-direction and puts all responsibility in the hands of the teacher engenders a psychological conflict in the adult learner, "and the typical method of dealing with psychological conflict is to try to flee from the situation causing it, which probably accounts in part for the high dropout rate in much voluntary adult education" (65). While student-veterans are used to taking orders, they are also accustomed to responsibility and respect. If they feel they do not have the respect of the teacher, they may disengage.

3. "The role of learners' experiences." This is a key principle, especially when applied to student-veterans. Knowles, Holton, and Swanson point out that adults tend to have a wider range of experiences than children, and that these experiences are tied to identity: "To children, experience is something that happens to them; to adults, experience is who they are. The implication of this fact for adult education is that in any situation in which the participants' experiences are ignored or devalued, adults will perceive this as rejecting not only their experience, but rejecting themselves as persons" (66–67). Adult educators should build upon adult students' experiences and individualize instruction to take those experiences into account. Knowles, Holton, and Swanson also caution that "as we accumulate experience, we tend to develop mental habits, biases, and presuppositions that tend to cause us to close our minds to new ideas, fresh perceptions, and alternative ways of thinking" (66).

4. "Readiness to learn." Knowles, Holton, and Swanson connect this principle to adults' real-life situations, stating that when adults feel a need to learn something new, that is the time to teach it to them. This principle seems tied to the first, "the need to know." However, the scholars

note that "it is not necessary to sit by passively and wait for readiness to develop naturally . . . There are ways to induce readiness through exposure to models of superior performance, career counseling, simulation exercises, and other techniques" (67)—in other words, to demonstrate a hitherto unfelt need to adult learners.

5. "Orientation to learning." Knowles and his coauthors call this point "critical" (67). Again, they connect adult learning to real-life situations, arguing that the subject-matter orientation of most schooling is inappropriate to adult students. They write that "in contrast to children's and youths' subject-centered orientation to learning (at least in school), adults are life-centered (or task-centered or problem-centered) in their orientation to learning" (67), and they suggest courses organized around the types of problems adults are likely to encounter and projects that replicate real-world applications of knowledge.

6. "Motivation." While Knowles, Holton, and Swanson acknowledge that adults are partially motivated extrinsically—seeking promotions and better jobs, for example—they argue that their primary motivators are intrinsic, such as self-esteem and quality of life.

One will note that several of these principles are similar and center on the acknowledgment and incorporation of adults' prior experience and felt needs into the curriculum. This seems not only respectful, but a good use of resources: as Knowles, Holton, and Swanson write, "For many kinds of learning, the richest resources for learning reside in the adult learners themselves" (2011, 66).

Persyn and Polson (2012) point out that adult learning theory has influenced the military's approach to training for many years: "The Army, Navy, Marine Corps, and Air Force have all integrated adult learning principles and theory to increase their organizations' effectiveness and address their learners' educational needs" (6). They provide examples that span literacy training during the Revolutionary War through modern training in critical thinking and problem solving. As they note, many of the military's educational practices explicitly draw from adult learning theory, incorporating self-directed learning, experiential education, and real-life situations.

The military's use of adult learning theory has also been noted by others. Urging military educators to adopt adult learning principles more fully, Carolyn Saunders (1991) argues that "we can implement an andragogical approach that is backed up by solid research that found that self-directed learning is the natural mode for adults, that adult students do possess the characteristics assumed in the andragogical model, and that learning does increase when this model is used" (42). Blaise Cornell-d'Echert (2012) writes:

If one of the new realities of 21st-century warfare is that everyone must think, preparation should offer military personnel of all ranks opportunity to practice thinking. This is all about problem solving. Too much military training (and doctrine-derived education) seeks to eliminate problems by providing learners with proven solutions to follow. It is efficient to train and test performance of military tasks as a measure of individual skill development. However, the reality of military performance is that military personnel receive and conduct missions. These missions are a series of problems that require solutions. Rarely are these missions a series of orchestrated tasks arranged in a logical sequence for careful monitoring by an outside observer. Fundamentally, military personnel are problem solvers. (21)

Like Saunders, Cornell-d'Echert argues that a strong connection to adult learning theory can help the military prepare its service members to carry out their tasks and reach their potential as learners and service members. Similarly, Zacharakis and Van Der Werff (2012) emphasize how the conscious incorporation of adult learning principles can help the military build critical-thinking capabilities in its ranks.

LEARNING IN THE MILITARY: IDENTITY, COMMUNITY, AND CRITICAL THINKING

Part of the mythos of military service is that it shapes one's identity. For those service members who enlist in their late teens, military service comes at a key formative period of late adolescence, often when a young man or woman is struggling to establish an adult identity separate from his or her family. The military can provide a new family, and with it, a new identity. As Amy said, "I loved every second of it. My favorite part was the camaraderie. It became a new family." When I asked Ryanne if she had any difficulties in the navy that she thought were related to her gender, she emphatically denied any, describing her male counterparts as "like brothers." Alan said that "everything [was] different" as a result of his time in the military. Derek credited his military service with changing his life. To some extent this is no surprise, since changing one's life is exactly what the military sets out to do. Doe and Doe (2013) note that "induction processes and follow-on military training function as forms of specialized literacy learning that leave a lasting imprint, often becoming central to the identity of the people who experience them" (para. 4).

A major part of this change has to do with forging a communal identity: as a veteran cited by Rumann and Hamrick (2010) says, "You become attached [to the soldiers in your unit]—they truly are your family" (446). Naphan and Elliott (2015) note that "the military operates through collective effort. For tasks to be accomplished and for individuals to survive within the military, putting the team ahead of oneself is necessary" (44). Other researchers, such as Morrow and Hart (2014), likewise emphasize the military's priority on building a cohesive team. As Derek said, "In the military you go through your training programs, [and] whether it's aircraft maintenance school or it's Special Forces school or noncommissioned officer school, everything is done as a team. Everything is done together. Nothing accomplished is ever done alone or individually." The emphasis on forging a cohesive team certainly makes sense. Most military service members will deploy as teams and carry out their work on the battlefield as teams; it is crucial for them to be able to work well with others. Accordingly, the military emphasizes teamwork and community not just on the battlefield, but throughout training.

Largely because of the often-chaotic nature of today's armed conflicts, much of the training in the armed forces also encourages critical thinking and problem solving at every level (not just for officers). For example, when writing about the marine corps's integration of critical-thinking preparation at all levels of training, Zacharakis and Van Der Werff (2012) state that "the goal is to develop a learning organization that is made of educated critical thinkers. All marines are expected to make a contribution to the team, not just with their ability to fire a rifle or follow orders but also through the ability to think, self-regulate their emotions, and take responsibility for their and the team's actions" (95). Hadlock and Doe (2014) point out that "the military has put more focus on decision making and agency at the individual and team level than ever before, and responsibility resides less and less exclusively in the senior leader" (79). Similarly, the Army Learning Concept for 2015 emphasizes the need "to develop higher-order thinking skills for all soldiers, ensuring they are prepared for the dynamic, complex, and ambiguous operational environments likely to face them in future conflicts" (Zacharakis and Van Der Werff 2012, 11). In short, service in the military now includes an expectation that service members at all levels will be able to contribute to the welfare and success of the organization with their brains, not just with their brawn.

Perhaps surprisingly to those of us in the academy, military training can incorporate a substantial amount of reading and writing. For example, here is how Mike described learning and demonstrating what he knew in the coast guard:

> MIKE: In the coast guard there's a lot of written tests and a lot of studying and hitting the books. For the coast guard, [for promotions] you get like five or six books for, like, mechanics. And then you have to take a

mechanics test. And then you get two or three books about the military uniforms and regulations and history and so forth. And then you have to take a test for that. And then after that, you take what's called a service-wide, where you compete with other people trying to get the same position you're getting. One time when I was taking the test, I think there was 500 people that were taking the test for the service-wide, but they were only going to promote about 70 people. So you take the test, which is 80 percent of your grade, and then they factor in your years of service, performance, and sea time, and other factors like that.

Some service members receive specialized writing training, depending on the work they do in the military. For example, Joseph wrote for army publications. After he enlisted, the army trained him in the specific forms of writing he would need to do his job:

JOSEPH: It was like you went to boot camp, and then you immediately went on to essentially writing boot camp. And while it wasn't artsy and it wasn't a freethinking environment per se, it definitely, like, forced me to hone the skills that I had and understand grammar a little better and understand how to produce something on a timeline.

Another example of specialized writing my participants learned was the "counseling report," or evaluation of their subordinates.

BRIAN: The idea behind it is to inform the soldier, to go over their career and what they were doing and what they need to work on, whether it's, you know, their military bearing, if they weren't being courteous or saying, "Yes, sir" or "No, Sergeant." Or standing at parade rest when they're speaking to higher-ranking NCOs or sergeants. Or how they were doing on physical fitness. You want to take a soldier, say, "This is what I see of you. This is what happened. This is what we need to work on. And this is what will help your career in the army." So the idea behind it is to create success in the soldiers.

According to Brian, soldiers learn the genre requirements of the counseling reports primarily from their superior officers. Sometimes they would explicitly lay out what they wanted step by step, but sometimes, Brian said, "You would get a vibe. The military is like kind of a subculture of its own. You kind of learn how to communicate without necessarily passing the words or whatever, you know what I mean?" Amy and Logan both said they learned how to write logs from models provided by, respectively, the marines and the navy; Amy learned how to write counseling reports from being counseled herself: "You picked that up from getting counseled yourself as a junior marine, so you know what it looks like." As others have illustrated, student-veterans' experience with writing was not limited to my study participants, but is relatively common throughout the military (Hadlock 2012; Hinton 2013).

The military also encourages in-depth examination of difficult issues through reading, writing, and group conversation. Logan still had several training documents from a 2008 navy "Pride and Professionalism Workshop" that outline scenarios in which participants are asked to problem-solve communication conflicts. For example, the *Trainee Guide* asks participants to break up into small groups and discuss the following scenario:

> A work center supervisor reprimands an Airman because the Airman did not complete a task the supervisor assigned him. The Airman begins to defend himself, but the supervisor cuts him off with, "I don't want any excuses! Just get back in there and get to work. And from now on do what I tell you *when* I tell you." Later, the work center supervisor's own supervisor approaches her and says, "Sorry for pulling Airman —— off the job yesterday, but I really needed him." (*Trainee Guide* 2008, 84)

The guide then asks groups to write responses to a series of questions about what specific aspects of communication broke down in the scenario and how the problems might be resolved. After the trainees compose their answers, they are asked to report back to the larger group, which then discusses responses from all the small groups. The instructor guide, which Logan also provided, emphasizes that "there are no absolutely right or wrong answers here. There are a number of problems in this scenario. The important thing is to get the trainees to think about the scenario, communication, and how breakdowns in communication can lead to conflict" (*U.S. Navy Pride and Professionalism* 2008, 1.3.10). These instructions underscore how the actual learning environment in the military is much richer than the popular reductive portrayals of drill instructors barking orders and enlisted men and women being instructed to shoot, not think.

"LEARNING SHOCK" AND THE DISCONNECT BETWEEN MILITARY AND ACADEMY

Some of the reasons student-veterans may have a difficult transition to college are that the community of practice framework does not work well in undergraduate education and andragogical principles are imperfectly understood and applied in college. Accordingly, student-veterans can experience a disruption as they transition from one learning environment to another that is similar to a culture shock. In a conversation about this transition, Louise Wetherbee Phelps termed this "learning shock," a phrase I think encapsulates the disorientation student-veterans can experience as they enter college.

As with culture shock, learning shock implies a past experience that is disconnected with the present and, at times, at cross-purposes with it. Frequently, higher education seems to treat student-veterans as though they come from a vacuum as far as learning is concerned—as though the time they spent between high school and college was a caesura during which learning did not happen. As should be evident from the previous sections, nothing is further from the truth. Success in the military is predicated on an aptitude for learning and, moreover, on the ability to internalize and apply knowledge in diverse, often high-stress situations. However, the learning environment and the theoretical underpinnings of the military differ from those that tend to be valued in academia. When student-veterans transition poorly from one learning environment to the other, their difficulties should be viewed in terms not of lack but of disconnect: they do not lack ability or experience learning new skills and information, but the way they are accustomed to doing so may not connect well with college.

Take communities of practice. A rich body of work focuses on supporting communities of practice among faculty and graduate students within disciplines—logical, since those individuals are already members of a clearly defined disciplinary community with similar interests and goals. (For some examples, see Crede, Borrego, and McNair [2010] on engineering grads, or Valentine [2009] on English graduate students in the writing center.) However, research on even advanced undergraduates is sparse. Commonly, scholars who have tackled this issue focus on some sort of capstone project undertaken by juniors or seniors that is specifically designed to prepare them for their disciplinary workplace—for example, a major senior project in an architectural design studio (Morton 2012), a final-year group project meant to simulate an information-technology consultancy (Fearon, McLaughlin, and Eng 2012), or a senior capstone design project in an engineering school in which the students develop and test an actual product (Dannels 2000).

The effectiveness of these communities of practice appears to be mixed. The most common challenge reported is that the students perceive the CoPs as artificial, more closely tied to school than to their disciplines or eventual workplaces. As Dannels (2000) writes, "The academic audience emerged as the central audience . . . [and students] focused on academic persons as their most central customers" (22). The scholars I cite above do not argue that the CoP framework will not work in school—on the contrary, all provide suggestions for how to fine-tune the projects to better mesh with the professional world. However, it seems reasonable to extrapolate that if students who are on the verge of graduation have difficulty seeing their schoolwork as directly tied to their disciplinary community of practice, this difficulty would be even more pronounced among students at the beginning of their college careers.

Indeed, Lave and Wenger (1991) intentionally steered clear of a focus on schooling in their foundational text. They write that schooling and the CoP framework are not necessarily incompatible, but that the learning that is expected to happen in school is often too generalized and abstract to mesh well with their theory of learning. As I noted at the beginning of this chapter, Lave and Wenger view learning as highly situated and occurring in a specific context; while they acknowledge that learning happens in schools, they raise questions about the connections between schools and the communities that originate the knowledge/practices that schools purport to teach. In other words, their concerns are similar to those of current scholars who critique our ability to teach academic discourse in writing classes: if discourses are situated, we can only teach an approximation of them when we remove them from their disciplinary context (a point strongly argued by Downs and Wardle [2007] and expanded upon by others).

Another problem with applying the CoP framework to undergraduate education is that entering students do not want to become full members of the academic community—unless, of course, their career goals are to become academics themselves. The student-veterans I interviewed had a variety of career goals, including law enforcement, business, and journalism. Their time in college, while important, was transitory: their goals were centered on becoming prepared to do their eventual jobs. This contrasts sharply with their goals in entering the military. All of the student-veterans I interviewed joined the service because they wanted to be service members. For example, Brian, a member of the fourth generation in his family to enlist in the army, stated that he enlisted primarily "to serve [his] country in her time of need." Alan wrote in his survey that he had "always idolized soldiers, especially trigger pullers. The best way to show respect is to do it yourself."

They may have had other goals as well, such as supporting their family (Mike) or paying for an eventual college education (Logan and Ryanne), but they all viewed the military as a community they wanted to join. In this they were likely similar to most other student-veterans. In terms of the CoP framework, they were motivated to become full participants in the military. While they want to do well in school, it is not because they want to become full participants in the academic CoP, but because doing well in school is a means to an end: landing a career.

In sum, the community of practice framework is a powerful tool for understanding how learners acquire the knowledge and practices of the military, but it is difficult to apply to undergraduate education. Additionally, as I noted earlier in this chapter, the military embraces andragogical principles, but few college courses are really designed with adult learners in mind. Instead, they are structured to teach traditional-age students, who are characterized (sometimes implicitly) as novices—not only to the subject matter, but to learning. This characterization is obviously erroneous when applied to veterans, who have a great amount of experience learning and applying new knowledge, and indeed a great amount of life experience that is useful in college.

Yet colleges tend to do a poor job taking student-veterans' prior experience into account, which can be particularly galling for them. For example, Logan expressed frustration that he was placed into developmental writing by a computer that, he felt, did not adequately understand his writer's voice. The placement was done by COMPASS, a standardized instrument that Logan believed did not take his experience into account. Joseph dropped his communication class because he felt that the first day's activity—a standard icebreaker—was juvenile and the instructor heckled him for not adequately buying into it. As Knowles, Holton, and Swanson (2011) argue, for adult learners, "experience is who they are. The implication of this fact for adult education is that in any situation in which the participants' experiences are ignored or devalued, adults will perceive this as rejecting not only their experience, but rejecting themselves as persons" (66–67). This was certainly the case with the veterans with whom I spoke, and it serves as a major caution to those of us who work with student-veterans: if we devalue their experiences, we run the risk of devaluing veterans themselves.

ADULT LEARNERS AND THE TRANSITION TO COLLEGE

Hart and Thompson (2013) write that "many of the transition issues that are reported by veterans parallel in significant ways the transition many non-traditional students face when making the move from careers back to college, suggesting the possibility that some of the transitional issues are less about their status as veterans and more about their status as adult learners" (4). As O'Donnell and Tobbell (2007) point out, "Adult students are potentially more vulnerable to difficulties in the management of [college] transitions because of their (often) minority status in [higher education], because they may have little recent experience of formal education, and because they may have additional life pressures out of university" (313). Also, many adult students at community colleges such as the one where I performed my research have not had ideal prior experiences with education; in my observation, this is often true with veterans, many of whom joined the military in part to pursue a career that did not require a college education. Now, they find themselves back in school and do not quite know how to proceed.

While keeping in mind the individuality of adult learners' experiences, it is still possible to make some generalizations about the group. For example, mature students tend to experience college differently from traditional students on an emotional level. A number of researchers have noted that adult students frequently have higher levels of anxiety than traditional students, especially in their first year of college (Navarre Cleary 2012). To be sure, many students experience anxiety when they enter college, especially in writing classes—for example, in a broad study of first-year students at CUNY, Zajacova, Lynch, and Espenshade (2005) found that out of twenty-seven possible college tasks, students ranked "writing term papers" as the most stressful (688). They also ranked writing papers as the activity in which they perceived they had the second-least self-efficacy, making paper-writing assignments a kind of perfect storm of misery.

For adult learners, though, writing anxiety can be even more acute. Navarre Cleary (2012) describes adult students who have anxiety about writing that is so intense they experience muscle spasms and mouth sores. In the students she describes, anxiety centers on "not knowing what to write because they had a hard time imagining the university and not knowing if they were writing well enough because they had a hard time imagining *themselves* in the university" (364; my emphasis). Navarre Cleary describes how one student, struggling with high-stakes writing assignments and little feedback, felt as though her prior experience did not apply to the academic world. Another performed much better, in large part because several low-stakes writing assignments with detailed feedback granted her entrance into the requirements of the academic discourse community.

However, even the best designed writing courses sometimes are not enough to counteract the negative self-images some adult learners have regarding their academic abilities or the disconnect they feel with traditional-age students. Bay (1999) describes two mature students whom she recommended for an honors section of composition: one, a veteran, elected not to take the course because he still saw himself as a poor writer (despite his excellent performance in the first semester of composition), and the other found younger students overly limited in their life experiences and so elected to take an independent study (308). Additionally, there is often a significant amount of time between when adult learners end their high-school careers and when they go to college, and they may worry (sometimes accurately) that they have forgotten key elements of academic writing in the interim. Navarre Cleary (2008) terms this "fear of brain rot" (115), and points out that while the anxiety some adult students feel that their brains have "atrophied beyond repair" is certainly exaggerated (115), their concern that college writing has requirements that are unknown and confusing to them is likely valid (116). She and others suggest that writing teachers can alleviate some of this anxiety (and encourage better writing from students) by being more explicit about our assignments, more detailed in our feedback, and by encouraging open conversations about the struggles we all have with writing.

Some student-veterans may feel more acute forms of anxiety than other adult students. A number of studies have found that anxiety is relatively common in student-veterans (Campbell and Riggs 2015; Rattray et al. 2019), and PTSD is also prevalent (Baechtold and De Sawal 2009; US Department of Veterans Affairs 2018). Campbell and Riggs (2015) found that social support ameliorated much of the potential negative effects of anxiety and depression in student-veterans, suggesting that robust college counseling centers and veteran support services (veteran liaisons and SVA clubs, for example) can help student-veterans succeed at college. Baechtold and De Sawal (2009) also suggest that college support services can help student-veterans deal with anxiety, PTSD, and culture shock. Still, we should be aware that student-veterans may be dealing with strong feelings of anxiety that could be related to fears about their ability to succeed at college.

Despite these challenges, adult learners can be some of the strongest students in a class. Like many teachers, I have typically found them to be hard workers who are extremely motivated to succeed. I rarely have to worry about them doing their homework, and on several occasions have been pleasantly surprised when they tell me they looked up a (nonrequired) reading or video I mentioned in class. Despite their frequent anxiety about their writing skills, they often become leaders in group work and mentor younger students academically and socially. My anecdotal findings are consistent with current scholarship. I have noted above that researchers have confirmed that adult students bring useful experience to higher education (Knowles, Holton, and Swanson 2011; Navarre Cleary 2008). They are also highly motivated (McGivney 2004; Navarre Cleary and Wozniak 2013; Taylor and House 2010)—in fact, that is one of the most consistent findings about adult learners. Some research indicates that this motivation is more intrinsic than in traditional-age students (Knowles, Hilton, and Swanson 2011; Taylor and House 2010). In contrast to younger students, many of whom attend college because their parents mandate it or it just seems like the thing to do after high school, adult learners have made a conscious choice to go back to school. Often this choice involves significant sacrifice, and adult learners are invested in making sure that sacrifice pays off.

However, the norms and expectations of higher education, including how to write successfully, can be difficult to understand. Theresa Lillis (2001) points out that "student academic writing constitutes a very particular kind of literacy practice which is bound up with the workings of a particular social institution" (39), and argues that the type of writing valued in school is not universal (or universally "good"), but rather tied to the values of higher education. She goes on to highlight the confusion experienced by post-traditional students as they begin to write essays, calling it "so all-pervasive . . . that it signals the need to look beyond a notion of individual confusion, towards an institutional practice of mystery" (53). Lillis does not allege that this mystery is intentional, but rather that the conventions of successful essay writing are so ingrained in the college community that they have become largely implicit. Teachers and tutors, "having been socialized into them through years of formal schooling, and in many cases through socio-discursive practices in their homes and communities" (75), often feel like these conventions are simply common sense and have difficulty putting into words what students need to do. Lillis argues that this serves to exclude from higher education those students—especially post-traditional students—who do not already have an implicit understanding of higher-education writing practices. Veterans would likely be particularly vulnerable to such exclusion.

LESSENING LEARNING SHOCK: SPECIFIC RECOMMENDATIONS

It is likely that many student-veterans will find the transition to college somewhat jarring no matter what we do. The academy is, in many ways, an odd and idiosyncratic community, and all students need to adapt and adjust as they enter it. Colleges are also slow to change, meaning that if they are to succeed, student-veterans will likely have to adapt more to college than college adapts to them. However, those of us who are classroom teachers often have a significant amount of flexibility in how we set up our learning environments, and a more informed understanding of the learning environment student-veterans are used to from their military experience can help us develop interventions to ease their transition. I provide several recommendations for writing teachers below.

Explore Community and Identity

As I noted above, veterans come from a sharply defined community of practice, and we will be unable to replicate such a community in college. However, we can (and should) examine the ways we understand community in college and writing classes. For example, consider how we structure mainstays of writing classes such as collaborative work. A number of studies have found that student-veterans tend to be frustrated by their civilian peers, mostly because of what they perceive as the civilians' lack of work ethic, unreliability, and superfluous concerns (e.g., Persky and Oliver 2010; Wheeler 2012). As Naphan and Elliott (2015) write, "While social cohesion served a valuable purpose in combat, the intensity of it at the time made it difficult later on for student veterans to feel like anyone in the civilian world, including at college, could understand them" (43). This frustration also came through in my interviews. For example, Logan described sitting in the library doing homework and getting increasingly frustrated listening to a nearby conversation between two other students about the television show *The Voice*.

> LOGAN: I couldn't believe how upset I was getting about how stupid the whole conversation was. They went on for an hour about this. I didn't have a very intense military career, I had a very enjoyable fun time out there, you know. But I'm just thinking of all the people out there who are risking their lives and stuff so people can be sitting around talking about Christina Aguilera until the ends of the earth, the types of pants she's wearing. It was a little aggravating.

Joseph described group work as "sometimes a social nightmare" because he thought that the other members of his group "wonder[ed] why your career track is starting later at college, which generates a hurdle that has to be overcome in most situations before a person can feel comfortable with you." Derek noted that in the military, he had become accustomed to people following through in group work. However, in college, "I don't know how many times . . . like endlessly with my classmates saying, 'Okay, I'll meet you at 2:00,' and we've got a final the next day. We're counting on each other to get through this stuff together, and they don't show up."

Ryanne also expressed frustration with the poor work ethic and unwillingness to follow through that she saw in her civilian peers. She was dismayed by "how narrow people's vision is" in regard to larger world issues, and went on to say, "It's a struggle to relate to people. I was really alone for a long time [when she got out of the navy] because I didn't relate to people my own age, people didn't have the same work ethic as me so I struggled with people at work . . . I really struggled to make friends as loyal as military people are." Amy also said that she has difficulty communicating with nonmilitary students and can be irritated at what she sees as their lack of respect for people with more experience and knowledge. For example, she described getting angry in class when she felt as though civilian students were not treating the professor with sufficient respect, and that her anger actually distracted her from the content of the class.

It seems clear that if we view our students overly simplistically and homogenize them into a group with relatively uniform experience, we will tend to assign collaborative work with the naive expectation that group interactions will somehow work themselves out naturally. This approach does a disservice to the variety present in all of our students, but it can be especially hard on our veterans. Highly structured expectations for collaborative work can help, since veterans are used to having group tasks with clear objectives. For example, if we assign peer response, we might consider also assigning specific roles within the group and clear objectives for what each group will accomplish.

We also need to remember that most student-veterans will not be long-term members of the academic community in the same way that they were (and, in the case of those who continue to serve, still are) in the military. Their time in college is transitional. This understanding should make us question why and how much we focus on strictly "academic" genres in our writing classes. Surely we can find room for writing that is more closely connected to the workplaces that our student-veterans hope to enter. Additionally, all students would likely be served by developing a deeper understanding of writing itself and how they can transfer their knowledge to disparate writing situations.

Borsari et al. (2017) note that student-veterans tend to "experience the push and pull of two identities—one as a veteran with unique experiences and a skill set different than that of the traditional student, the other as a student trying to integrate and adapt in the college" (168). Connected to this, a key point that we need to remember is that we are asking student-veterans to become "student-like" rather than abandon their prior identities: we want them to connect to college and their professors and perform the student role well enough to succeed. As I have noted throughout this chapter, veterans share many things in common with other adult post-traditional students, and this struggle to incorporate a student identity is a good example. As O'Donnell and Tobbell (2007) point out in their discussion of adult returning students,

> In transition, the notion of identity is in the foreground because the new and strange practices force reconsideration of practice and therefore shifts in identity trajectories. The nature of the individual trajectory is constructed through the interaction of the past, present, and perhaps future aspirations of the student . . . Past failures in the education system, combined with non inclusionary practices in the HE institution may be in opposition to aspirations of educational success and serve to generate meanings that shape identity in a certain and not necessarily advantageous way. (315)

This quote is particularly relevant to student-veterans. Many of my participants related they'd had "past failures in the education system" as well as a general lack of interest in high school. A central challenge to schools and faculty is to demystify educational practices so that veterans (and other post-traditional students) can more clearly see how they can participate productively in higher education.

In conversations with student-veterans, writing teachers can help them understand that a successful student identity is, to a large extent, a role they are performing. We must take care not to diminish the significance or importance of that role; however, it is still a role. As Burgess and Ivanič (2010) write, identity is

> not unitary or fixed but has multiple facets; is subject to tensions and contradictions; and is in a constant state of flux, varying from one time and one space to another. This multifaceted identity is constructed in the interaction between a person, others, and their sociocultural context. It includes the "self" that a person brings to the act of writing, the "self" she constructs through the act of writing, and the way in which the writer is perceived by the reader(s) of the writing. (232)

Several researchers have noted that writers align themselves with communities through writing; as Herrington and Curtis (2000) put it, college writers look for people, languages, genres, and practices "with which to shape a self to speak from . . . Also important, as these students were developing the sense of a kindred group to speak *from*, they were simultaneously envisioning a group they spoke *for*, a group with whom they also shared an identity" (370–371).

In other words, writers perform identities that connect them to their discourse communities—what Roz Ivanič (1998) calls a writer's "discoursal self." As Ivanič points out, this is a *persona*, a role that students adopt to show membership. Scholars such as Donna LeCourt (2006) have explored identity performance in terms of working-class students who are concerned about leaving their home identities behind; research such as this can be extrapolated to shed light on the identity performances of student-veterans. LeCourt argues that the conception of identity as "always under construction, always being negotiated, and always felt and enacted in relation to other classes, discourses, and power structures" can help students become aware of how they continually construct their class identities (45). Again, we can probably extrapolate this to student-veterans—not only because many veterans, especially at the community college level, come from working-class backgrounds, but because they are entering a community that seems to ask them to completely and immediately reshape themselves. We can help them understand that this is not actually the case.

Integrate Adult Learning Theory

Improving faculty members' familiarity with adult learning theory would benefit all students, but, as Navarre Cleary and Wozniak (2013) argue, it is especially important if we want to help student-veterans. One reason is that, as I noted above, the military itself embraces adult learning theory, and doing so in college can reduce veterans' learning shock. But it also can suggest ways to understand and support some of the characteristic difficulties veterans experience when they enter college. The field of adult learning theory is broad, but a good place to start is Malcolm Knowles's six principles of andragogy (Knowles, Holton, and Swanson [2011], discussed earlier in this chapter): the need to know, the learners' self-concept, the role of learners' experiences, readiness to learn, orientation to learning, and motivation. Of these six concepts, I would argue that writing teachers in particular should start with the need to know, the learners' self-concept, and the role of learners' experiences.

The first concept, the need to know, describes how adult learners are unlikely to take the teacher's word that something is important; instead, they want to know the potential benefits and drawbacks associated with learning the material. Knowles, Holton, and Swanson (2011) recommend that teachers incorporate simulations or scenarios that will let learners discover gaps between where they currently are with the material and where they want to be. To this, I would add that a wise course for writing teachers would be to examine the curricula of their courses with an eye toward how they can demonstrate the usefulness of what they are teaching. Unfortunately, we too often ask students to trust that a given essay or assignment will pay off several years down the road; this can be especially hard for student-veterans, who are used to clear objectives. Because they are diligent, motivated students, they will probably do the work no matter what we tell them. However, if we can provide them with clear rationales for our assignments and requirements, we can tap into the well of intrinsic motivation that resides within many student-veterans.

Second, the learners' self-concept is particularly important when we work with student-veterans. The veterans in our classes have been accustomed to bearing a great deal of responsibility and, oftentimes, authority over others. They are expert sonar technicians, tank commanders, and aircraft mechanics, and many times they have been all over the world. We do them a great injustice when we treat them like eighteen-year-olds who are just leaving home for the first time. When possible, we should engage their maturity and experience by involving them in directing their own learning. For example, I suggested above that veterans respond well to direct feedback and clear expectations; when we give them, we can also lay out options for them to address any writing difficulties and work with them to develop their own plan to improve. We are the experts in writing, a fact they will readily acknowledge; however, they are the experts in how they learn, and we need to acknowledge that as well.

Encourage Connection through Mindful Abstraction

Knowles, Holton, and Swanson (2011) urge us to build on learners' experiences with our curriculum, and this seems particularly important with veterans. It also seems very attainable in most writing classes. For example, Mike talked about how he wrote almost twice as much as the requirement in his assignment on sexual harassment in the military, and that he "kind of had an advantage there over people in my class because none of them have been in the military." If student-veterans have self-disclosed their veteran status in a course, we can ask if they mind being called on when course topics touch on the military or world events. We can encourage them to journal about their time in the military, or ask them to make connections between what they learned in the military and what they are learning in school. We can talk with them about how some of the habits they learned in the service set them up well for college success and support their transfer of those skills. In short, we can demonstrate that their time in the military has value in the academic world.

The term I like for these types of activities is "mindful abstraction," which I draw from research on transfer theory. Perkins and Salomon

(1988) helpfully divide knowledge transfer into two general types: low-road, which addresses more automatic transfer of simple concepts, and high-road, which focuses on big-picture, complex knowledge. As Brent (2011) points out, much research on transfer suggests that asking students to mindfully abstract knowledge—in other words, think, write, and talk about what they have learned and how they might apply it in other contexts—can greatly improve students' ability to transfer knowledge. I think that a similar principle applies to learning contexts. As I noted earlier in this chapter, enlisted service members are asked to think critically, debate courses of action, and respond to complex scenarios. Many are also asked to read challenging texts and discuss them, and as they advance in rank, they are asked to write more as well. Asking them to mindfully abstract not just *what* they learned, but *how* they learned is likely to increase their ability to make a strong transition to college. I explore this concept more in chapters 3 and 4.

CONCLUSION

Many of our students have difficulty making the transition to college and meeting the expectations of academic discourse. It should come as no surprise that student-veterans also frequently find this transition jarring. Exploring ways in which student-veterans can leverage their military mindsets and identities for college success can help. While many veterans will likely see the military and the academy as completely separate, we can help them think about how, for example, approaches to problem-solving and a team orientation developed in the military can be advantageous in college. Integration of andragogy is also extremely important, as student-veterans are post-traditional students who need to have their life experience acknowledged and valued.

2

STRENGTHS OF THE
VETERAN MINDSET

While it is true that many student-veterans find the transition to college difficult, their time in the military is also likely to have imparted traits that can facilitate college success. For example, they have been trained to be leaders and mutually reliant team members (Morrow and Hart 2014). They tend to be mission-focused, trained to persist over long periods of time in difficult situations. Many student-veterans have a more developed and nuanced worldview than most traditional students, a result of working with diverse people in the military and experiencing different cultures around the world, and they can bring this experience to bear in class discussions and papers (Morrow and Hart 2014; Schell and Kleinbart 2014). An American Council on Education (2011) report also found that student-veterans defined success more broadly than many traditional students, and Hart and Thompson (2013) note that "most faculty report . . . a high sense of initiative, professionalism, and leadership" (4).

In response to Hart and Thompson's (2013) argument that much student-veteran research and training is grounded in a deficit mindset, I asked my participants to identify any strengths they thought might be characteristic of the student-veteran population. Every participant was able to quickly generate a list, and there were clear trends across interviews. Strengths that the participants identified, as well as those that emerged through coding, guided the organization of the next sections of this chapter. Three key strengths emerged: a drive to complete the mission, an enriched understanding of the world and its citizens, and a connection to the larger community. After exploring these strengths in the context of my interview data, I contextualize them with current scholarship on student retention and success. As was the case with the preceding chapter, this chapter ends with specific recommendations for how colleges can build on veterans' strengths to aid them in their college transitions.

DOI: 10.7330/9781646421343.c002

A DRIVE TO COMPLETE THE MISSION

Several veterans I interviewed highlighted the military's emphasis on "completing the mission" as a principal strength of student-veterans. In the academic context, "completing the mission" could mean completing an assignment, class, or degree program; this was a connection between the military and academic worlds that several veterans made explicitly. For example, one of Alan's first classes was speech. Fresh from serving in Iraq, he presented an informative speech about the region; his instructor, a middle-aged male who did not have a history of military service, stopped him in the middle and "corrected" Alan's pronunciation of the country's name, which greatly angered Alan. When Alan later sent an email to his instructor about the situation, he felt as though the instructor brushed him off. Despite his anger at the instructor and his distaste for the course, Alan refused to give up. In his interview, he connected his persistence to his military training: he saw finishing the course as a contest between himself and his instructor; dropping the class would mean his instructor would win. Alan said that he would never give up, because in the military, if you gave up, the enemy would win. Alan argued that other veterans who had been trained for the battlefield would feel the same—they would never give up.

Joseph characterized the military's emphasis on completing the mission similarly.

> JOSEPH: That's something that I think is paramount to what the military forces you to do. I mean, you're really required to always finish the mission. I mean, that's not only, it's not only an idea—in the army it's one of our warrior ethoses: "I will put the mission first." And when you translate that into the academic world or, say, a degree, if you can use those skills of putting the mission first in academics, it definitely helps you to get your job done, to think of things like deadlines or turn-in dates or upcoming exams as objectives. I think that's a definite advantage.

Hinton (2013, 2014) notes that motivation and commitment are often explicitly taught in military training courses in addition to being embedded in the general military culture. Certainly, Brian wrote that his time in the army "taught me the value of a good work ethic." He elaborated on this in his interview:

> BRIAN: I think the biggest thing, the biggest aspect, I learned in the army is to aggressively pursue what needs to be done. So if I had an issue or trouble with something [in college], I would be able to seek out how to fix it or how to figure out how to do it. So whether it's by finding it myself or finding someone who knows how I would need to write something better, or finding information on something I need to

write about. That's what I would say I drew from the military: I could, like, buckle down and get it done.

Derek touched on this topic as well. In his interview, he stated that "the military taught me how to study, how to work hard, discipline." Ryanne described herself as developing a "wicked work ethic" in the navy: "I'm very goal-driven. I know what I want, and I'm not afraid to go after it."

Amy, who went to college for a year before enlisting in the marines, described a sharp difference in how she approached school before and after her service. Prior to the marines, she had a hard time getting up on time and making it to class. She didn't take college seriously and found it challenging to follow through on tasks. According to her, five years in the marines completely changed this mindset: "They instill time management in you. You need to get up and get where you're supposed to be and get things done. In the marine corps, if you're not fifteen minutes early, you're late." Amy was able to take this work ethic to college and found that she worked harder than many of her civilian peers.

Similarly, Mike noted that "overall, I'd say I spend more time on the subjects than the other students do, but I think I have a higher attention to detail as part of my training and maybe personality."

> MIKE: I didn't have the skills to learn how to learn [in high school], so I really didn't learn how to learn until I went into the military. And in the coast guard there's a lot of written tests and a lot of studying and hitting the books. So that's really where I learned how to learn. If I went to college after high school, I would have just wasted my time and my money. I wasn't disciplined enough.

One way Mike developed this discipline and connected it to academics was in preparing for the "service-wide" tests for promotion that are offered in the coast guard. Mike reported studying for six months for his service-wide tests, primarily reading books and manuals, which he thought helped him prepare for the reading and studying demands of college.

This focus on discipline, completing the mission, and working hard has been noted by other researchers. Lighthall (2012) argues that student-veterans "work tirelessly to achieve their objectives" (89), and Wheeler (2012) writes that the student-veterans she spoke with made a direct connection between the work ethic they had developed in the military and their success in college. In her study, two veterans noted that in the military, relaxation always comes after training is completed, so they found it relatively easy to set up rules for themselves of homework first, downtime second. Other veterans told Wheeler that in the military they had learned to manage their time better or deal with stress, or that the "dedication and discipline" they had developed in the military helped them complete their schoolwork (782). Additionally, two veterans stated that "each assignment represented a mission so they approached them the same way they did in the service. First they planned the task, completed it to the best of their abilities, and learned from the outcome" (782).

In his essay about his own transition to college after his military service, Martin (2012) writes that "discipline and determination built into my character were instrumental in helping me make up the gaps formed by disability and insecurity" (28). This resonates with one of the strongest findings in Rumann and Hamrick's (2010) study: that student-veterans are more motivated and focused than the general student population. They wrote that the student-veterans with whom they spoke "described themselves as more mature, with clearer perspectives and increased goal commitment" (442). In addition to attributing this increased motivation and organization to their experience with military culture, some veterans in Rumann and Hamrick's study also noted that their service helped them understand what is important in life, or illustrated for them that without an education, they would likely have a less fulfilling career. While some of their respondents noted that they felt left behind by their nonmilitary peers, many also reported that this provided them with an increased clarity when it came to goals and motivation: in other words, they wanted to catch up.

AN ENRICHED UNDERSTANDING OF THE
WORLD AND ITS CITIZENS

Rumann and Hamrick (2010) found that most veterans who participated in their research also characterized themselves as "more interested in and more accepting of others" (448), and that they connected that openness to diversity within the armed services and the broad cultural experiences they had during deployment. This is similar to what I found in my research. Ryanne, for example, who grew up in an "isolated" small town, was stationed in Hawaii, where, she said, she "basically grew up." In her interview, she discussed how she had traveled all over the world during her service and was able to connect her world experience to her classes, specifically to sociology and psychology. On his survey, Brian noted that his "military service gave me a greater understanding of how society operates. [It gave me] exposure to people from all over the country—races, religions." Logan expressed something similar:

LOGAN: Since enlisting I feel more worldly. The navy got me out of [my
hometown] and out into the world abroad. I got to live in Hawaii,
California, and Cuba, and visited somewhere around another thirty-
ish countries. I feel the military gave me firsthand experience of other
places and people from all over the country and the world. It has been
a wonderful experience in contrast to growing up in homogenous
Northern Michigan.

It seems reasonable to think that student-veterans could build on this
worldliness not only as a source of material in a writing class and as a
lens through which to develop more nuanced and in-depth arguments
and positions, but also to interact better with the wide variety of students
and faculty at college.

Mike gave some specific examples of how his military experience
had given him material for his writing projects, helping him write
authoritatively about current issues and develop his essays beyond the
minimum requirements:

MIKE: We've had two essays due in our English class. One was "What
would you carry if you had to go to Afghanistan? What would [you]
take with you?" And then the other one we did yesterday was about
sexual harassment in the military. And both times we were provided a
news chapter. So I kind of had an advantage there over people in my
class because none of them have been in the military. Like yesterday
I wrote a paper and she wanted about 300 words, and I wrote almost
about 500 words. And it was for that sexual harassment in the military
but I [knew] so much about the subject in conjunction with the chapter so that's why it took me longer.

Hart and Thompson (2013) found that many of the faculty they
surveyed "remarked on the value of the varied cultural experiences
and broader world views that veterans tend to bring to class discussions and writing assignments" (4). Their point was similar to Street's
(2014) observations in the *Chronicle* that veterans provide a helpful
counterpoint to the perspectives of more traditional students. One of
the veterans Gann (2012) interviewed described a writing course he
had taken as being "more geared towards discussion, world views" and
stated that because of his military experience, he "was the only one
with any kind of knowledge about what was going on in the world or
politics" (223). Keast (2013) notes that explicitly encouraging student-
veterans to share their experiences and expertise that they have drawn
from their time in service can help them feel more connected to college, and that many veterans have told him that their experiences tend
to be "overlooked, undervalued, or unappreciated by civilian society"
(para. 23).

Hinton (2013) also points out that while student-veterans may be novices when it comes to academic writing, "they still retain expertise in many other areas and, as such, have experiences, beliefs, and habits that are valuable in the composition classroom" (para. 52). Hinton goes on to say that it is incumbent on writing teachers to craft classroom environments and assignments that provide space for veterans to apply this experience. It seems logical to expand her recommendation beyond the writing classroom and encourage teachers in all subjects to make this space.

A CONNECTION TO THE LARGER COMMUNITY

The veterans in this study often had difficulty connecting with their non-military peers, a finding that is consistent with other research (Borsari et al. 2017; Gann 2012; Wheeler 2012). However, this does not mean they had no desire to connect with anyone. The military is a social environment: most objectives are accomplished in teams. My interviews revealed that student-veterans are constantly on the lookout for other "teammates" to help them accomplish their objectives. Several spoke of how important other individuals had been to their success in college, or to their investment in writing. A number of veterans mentioned pivotal experiences early in their academic careers when teachers had taken extra time with them or told them that they had potential. Many also identified other veterans who had mentored them, or even whom they had mentored themselves. Some also talked about connections they had made with teachers or advisors on campus. They came off as far from isolated—in fact, they frequently sought out connections with other veterans, faculty, and advisors.

Alan said that he thought a smaller college and small classes were vital for veterans' success, precisely because they provided lots of opportunities for personal connections. He brought up a friend of his—an intelligence officer whom he characterized as very smart—who went to a big school after the service and dropped out because he felt lost in the crowd. In contrast, Alan has felt that the vast majority of his professors have cared about him and knew who he was. Ryanne similarly spoke highly of the small-college experience, citing a student-veteran friend who had an isolating experience in a larger school. She noted that the veteran affairs liaison at the college was especially important and felt like this person knew her and helped her remember to fill out her paperwork on time, enroll in classes, and more. She loved this personal connection.

When Joseph thought back on his time at community college, he also identified small classes and personal connections with his professors as keys to his success.

> JOSEPH: [The professors] were great. And they really kind of spring-boarded me back into the university, got me excited about going back to school. So I think that part of it is having small classrooms and having interactions with the students. If you get a veteran and he gets put in a group of 400 people and you break it down to groups of 10 or something, it can be really . . . you're out there on an island, not only socially, you're out there like actually academically on an island. I think having a little bit of one-on-one interaction is good for all students. And I think it's good for anybody that's trying to assimilate and having maybe an issue with that.

As a founder of Student Veterans of America, Derek has devoted a large amount of time and energy to helping student-veterans connect with one another. He noted that he could count on other student-veterans to show up for study groups and to help each other succeed at school. He identified this social support as often crucial to veterans' success in college.

> DEREK: [Student veterans might underestimate their abilities] without someone sitting down and telling them, "Hey, you should really take a look at this." Or "You should take a look at this school or this program" or "You should take these classes." Unless someone's really sitting them down and, like, hammering into their heads "You're capable of anything you want to do. It's just a matter of realizing that," they don't understand their potential and capabilities.

All students can probably benefit from an increased connection to their instructors and peers, but for student-veterans, such connections may be even more important. In her case studies of student-veterans, Gann (2012) writes that one of her participants (a former marine) found that "college is probably the most selfish environment you could ever encounter" (224); this student found it hard to understand how "there is no socially imposed impetus to help out another student who was struggling academically or socially" (224), and noted how different this was from his experience in the marines, where community support was ingrained in the culture. This student's observations paralleled Derek's characterization of the different approaches to peer support between the military and the academy:

> DEREK: In the military you go through your training programs, [and] whether it's aircraft maintenance school or it's Special Forces school or noncommissioned officer school, everything is done as a team. Everything is done together. Nothing accomplished is ever done alone

or individually. But when you come onto campus, it's number one first. There is no real sense of making sure that your colleagues make it through. It's all about making sure *you* make it through.

Martin (2012) also found that "a proclivity for teamwork and community-building is certainly a strength that results from military service" (30), and he described a successful mentoring program he set up wherein veterans new to the college environment were paired with more experienced student-veterans, either in the veteran organization or in their junior or senior year. Colleges would do well to harness the desire for teamwork and connection exhibited by many student-veterans to increase their connections with the college, their instructors, and each other, thereby setting them up for increased retention and success—as discussed in the next section.

CONNECTIONS WITH STUDENT-SUCCESS SCHOLARSHIP

The strengths of student-veterans that I noted above mesh well with current research on student retention and persistence, suggesting that veterans enter college with many skills that set them up for success rather than failure. For example, the student-veterans in this study characterized themselves as highly motivated and possessing a strong work ethic. They were convinced that they could get tasks completed, and they had a strong sense of discipline. Another way to describe these skills and self-concepts is to say that student-veterans have a strong sense of self-efficacy, and a number of researchers have connected students' sense of self-efficacy to college success.

The link between self-efficacy and student success is primarily indebted to the work of Bean and Eaton (2001). These researchers developed a model for predicting student success based on psychological factors such as intent, coping skills, and locus of control. Bean and Eaton theorized that students with well-developed self-efficacy and an internal locus of control (among other factors) were more likely to be successful at college, a model that has been confirmed through subsequent studies. For example, in a study of information systems students, Weng, Cheong, and Cheong (2010) found that student self-efficacy and commitment to goals were the top two determinants of whether students decided to stay in college or withdraw. Their findings were similar to those of Close and Solberg (2008), who studied the retention and success of Latino youth. Close and Solberg write that "positive academic outcomes result in large part by the student's level of academic self-efficacy. Defined as one's confidence to successfully execute or perform specific school-related activities, research has consistently found that higher levels of self-efficacy are associated with higher levels of achievement" (32). Some research has suggested that academic self-efficacy is particularly important to the success of adult post-traditional students; however, many adult students experience anxiety and apprehension upon returning to school, which reduces their sense of self-efficacy (O'Neill and Thompson 2013). The fact that student-veterans enter college with a high degree of self-efficacy can confer a distinct advantage.

The field of student retention and success also draws heavily on the work of Tinto (1987), which connects to the present discussion because of his focus on student integration. Tinto's model for student retention argues that students who are academically and socially well integrated in their college institutions are more likely to succeed (Stuart, Rios-Aguilar, and Deil-Amen 2014). This model has been found to be robust and predictive in multiple follow-up studies, although the relative influence of social and academic integration has been questioned: for example, some scholars argue that social integration is less important at community colleges (Stuart, Rios-Aguilar, and Deil-Amen 2014). Others argue that the importance of the two factors varies with the age of the student, with academic integration being more important to younger students and social integration gaining importance as students age (Mertes and Hoover 2014). Deil-Amen (2011) has suggested that for community college students, the social and the academic tend blend, and that it may be less useful to separate the two than in a university setting. Again, though, both types of integration have been shown through numerous studies to correlate with student success.

Student integration connects to veterans both in terms of strengths and challenges. As I noted earlier in this chapter, one key strength of student-veterans is that they seek out connections to supportive college personnel and other veterans. Such connections, especially those with college personnel, can lead to increased academic integration in college—and, in fact, that was what several of my participants reported. Connections with faculty or student services personnel not only helped them master course material and make sure they were getting their VA benefits, such connections also helped them feel as though they were a welcome part of the college community. In this, they are similar to other post-traditional adult students: research suggests that strong connections with instructors can lead to student persistence in college (O'Neill and Thompson 2013). Connections with other veterans, whether informally, as in Alan's case, or through the local chapter of the Student Veterans of America (SVA), helped lessen social isolation and increase social integration. However, we should strive to help student-veterans connect with nonveterans as well. This will help them feel as though they are true members of the college community.

As I noted in earlier sections, a key strength identified by my study participants was a greater knowledge of the world. In many ways, this was consistent with other adult post-traditional students, who tend to come to college with more life experience than traditional students. Wyatt (2011) argues that "prior knowledge and life experience is not only a crucial part of the contributions that post-traditional students bring to the classroom but paramount to the post-traditional students' successful engagement in the college environment" (14). This connects strongly with research on adult learning theory, especially Knowles's contention that adults' experiences are vital to their identities (Knowles, Holton, and Swanson 2011, 66–67).

Most college personnel would protest that they do not ignore or devalue veterans' experiences. However, college tends to be structured to serve younger, traditional students, and as a result, colleges and their courses do, in fact, tend to minimize adult learners' prior knowledge. In the case of veterans, this minimization is particularly unfortunate as it leaves untapped a resource that could enrich many college classes. While it is true that many student-veterans have been out of formal schooling for some time and that they will likely find many of the practices and structures of college strange, they bring skills to the table that can assist with that transition.

SPECIFIC INTERVENTIONS

The following recommendations build explicitly on the three key strengths listed above—veterans' drive to complete the mission, their enriched understanding of the world and its citizens, and their desire to connect—and they represent possible points that could be addressed in staff trainings and professional development workshops to help college personnel become more aware of how to build on these strengths. Additionally, I make several suggestions for how different areas of the college might support student-veterans' strengths through modifying or creating written guides, organizing veteran events, and more.

Clarify the Mission

Oftentimes, college personnel—especially faculty—have spent their entire careers in academia. Focusing on writing studies, Lillis (2001) has argued that there are so many understandings of and expectations for college writing that remain unspoken that it amounts to "an institutional practice of mystery" (53), a provocative characterization that I found my mind circling back to throughout the process of writing this book. This mystery goes beyond writing studies; in fact, it permeates colleges. Such mystery can be challenging for many students, but it can be especially so for student-veterans, who are used to clear expectations. Colleges can build on their work ethic and desire to "complete the mission" by clarifying that mission—in other words, by explicitly spelling out the ways colleges and courses work, and how veterans can succeed. Consider this quote from Brian:

> BRIAN: We're used to reading, you know, instructions or manuals. Depending what your job is, like, I was infantry, which isn't really that complicated. But we would have the old manual 7-7, which is basically the field manual for infantry. And it would go over basic stuff like weapons, team movement, which is how you move in a formation, whether it's in the field or how you cross roads, stuff like that, all the way up to, like, platoon squad size. And then there's more manuals that get up to, like, higher organizational, so platoon, company, battalion, brigade, stuff like that. But I'm sure military police will have their own manual or construction guys will have their own manual or tankers, truck drivers. Each vehicle comes with a manual. And it's really generic in terms of vehicle. So everything's in the same sections, like how you start it or how you do your pre-mission checks on it, where to check the oil . . .

Brian suggested that the college create a series of manuals for student-veterans that spelled out expectations and how to get help. He stressed that these manuals should focus on how to succeed academically, not just on how to obtain financial aid or enroll in classes.

Such manuals are an excellent idea, and they suggest relatively easy changes that colleges can implement immediately. Student services personnel and directors of writing centers and tutoring services could develop one-page guides to their services. Similarly, academic deans could lead efforts to construct similar materials for academic success. Such materials should be short, direct, and quick to comprehend, and they could be distributed to incoming student-veterans at orientations.

Brian's point about the military's emphasis on standardization is also a good one that we can learn from in the academy. Faculty members tend to deeply value their academic freedom and resist efforts to standardize materials between courses and faculty. However, when we consider the intellectual work students have to do to learn what is required in each class as they shift between instructors, we may begin to think that some amount of standardization might be a good thing.

We can learn from the military's emphasis on standardized formats. As Brian noted, an MP's job is different from a trucker's or an infantryman's, but each job has its own manual, and they are all organized the same way. In the academy, we could standardize the organization of writing prompts, course websites, syllabi, and other common materials—not the content, but the organization, so as to enable our students to find what they need and get the job done. We could also focus on being more direct with our wording and explicit about what it takes to succeed in each class.

Encourage Connections to Veterans' Experience

We should never put veterans on the spot in class discussions or other public forums by asking them to share their perspective on an issue "as a veteran." We should also keep in mind that every veteran is an individual, and it is as unfair to ask one to speak for the overall class of military personnel as it would be to ask a single person of color to speak for all people of color.

However, it is indeed possible to let student-veterans know that we welcome their perspectives and encourage any connections they might make between their military experience and course materials. Thompson (2014) provides a valuable list of suggestions to faculty for how to work with student-veterans on potentially controversial classroom topics such as war. Many of Thompson's suggestions center on the recommendation that faculty learn more about the military and the veteran experience, and that they work with student-veterans on an individual basis to see what they are comfortable sharing and what they are not. Some veterans—such as Mike, who drew from his experiences in the coast guard to enrich his English papers—will choose to bring their military experience into the classroom publicly. Others may not.

A good way for faculty members to start is by learning as much as one can about student-veterans as a group and as individuals. Vaccaro (2015) notes that student-veterans largely appreciate it when educators ask for perspectives on their time in the military and their transition to college. As Hart and Thompson (2016) write, encouraging student-veterans to share their experiences with professional writing and the larger world can greatly enrich the experiences of more traditional college students. Especially in a small, rural community college like my own, the contributions of a student who has seen more of the world than just the Midwest can be invaluable. However, we should, in general, refrain from calling on student-veterans to represent "the veteran perspective" in any debate for reasons stated above, and professors or other college personnel should be sure to respect student-veterans' choice not to share their status or experiences.

Create Resource Communities

Many student-veterans will respond well to the local chapter of SVA. Certainly, we can help new student-veterans by connecting them with the college's chapter, as advocated by Evans, Pellegrino, and Hoggan (2015). Most colleges also employ faculty and staff who are veterans themselves, and such college personnel could serve as excellent resource people for student-veterans.

However, those of us who are not veterans can also help. Many of the veterans I interviewed commented on how much they valued the connections they made with professors, regardless of whether those professors had served in the military. As Joseph stated, having a class that is small and intimate can help veterans feel as though they are less isolated and lead to success. Some scholars have found that student-faculty connections are particularly important at the community college level, not only in terms of helping students integrate into the college community, but in helping them overcome obstacles to success (Deil-Amen 2011). Evans, Pellegrino, and Hoggan (2015) also stress the value of faculty mentoring, even when those faculty are not veterans themselves.

As I noted earlier in this chapter, veterans tend to desire connection—including connections with nonveterans. They come from a team environment in which they learned to mutually support one another, and many find college's emphasis on the individual to be disheartening. We can build on their desire for connection by forming (or even leading) student-veteran study groups. Many veterans find what they see as the superficial concerns and lax work ethic of traditional-aged college students to be irritating—but they may connect better with the motivated post-traditional students who tend to abound at community colleges. Study groups and classroom teams that mix student-veterans and highly motivated returning students are worth exploring.

When administrators and student service personnel think about how to create formal venues for veterans to interact, they would do well to consider that student-veterans share many of the characteristics of other post-traditional adult learners (Navarre Cleary and Wozniak 2013). Adult learners tend to be highly motivated; they are also extremely busy and oftentimes juggling school as one of a number of important priorities

(Navarre Cleary 2008). Because of these time pressures, student-veterans will be less likely to show up at an event that does not seem to connect directly with their academic goals. In other words, while they might not attend a "veteran appreciation party," they probably would come to a study group or tutoring session that they saw as firmly connected to their college success. This hypothesis was supported by Deil-Amen's (2011) findings that for community college students, the social and the academic are often blended more than for traditional students, and that "social integration was often characterized by academic utility" (82). When applied to student-veterans, this research suggests that events that blend social connection and academic support might be effective ways to help student-veterans integrate (and succeed) at college.

CONCLUSION

Many colleges are responding to the influx of veterans by improving their veteran services and holding training workshops, but too often student-veterans are approached from a deficit mindset—we focus on what they lack rather than on what they bring to college. A more effective approach would take into account student-veterans' strengths and explore ways colleges can change to help veterans build on those strengths. This approach is consistent with Hart and Thompson's (2016) argument. Clarifying the often tacit understandings of college and course requirements, connecting course materials to veterans' experiences, and strengthening and expanding veteran resource communities are three key ways colleges can build upon student-veterans' strengths and improve their chances of college success.

3
WRITING IN THE MILITARY

Many writing faculty operate from the assumption that student-veterans did little or no writing in the military, or that their military experience has little bearing on their current work in writing classes. This is untrue. As my interviews illustrate, enlisted service members do, indeed, write during their time in the military, and they are quite aware of the processes whereby they learn the genre characteristics of that writing. In this chapter, I draw from a faculty survey to provide an example of how writing teachers commonly conceive of student-veterans' prior writing. I also draw from the veterans' interviews and examples of military writing to provide a sense of how veterans actually write in the military. These examples serve two purposes: first, to help interested readers develop a better sense of the military writing environment, and second, to lay the groundwork for some suggestions as to how we can help veterans build on their military writing experience to succeed in the academic context.

FACULTY UNDERSTANDINGS

When we explore student-veterans' transition to college writing, the veterans themselves are only part of the equation (albeit an important part!). The college environment, and particularly regarding student-veterans' writing classes, also plays a role. Accordingly, in addition to interviewing and surveying student-veterans—which I discuss in detail in "Introduction and Methodology"—I performed a small survey of the NCMC writing faculty. I sent a survey both electronically and in hard copy to all nineteen current writing faculty at NCMC (excluding myself). Of those faculty, four were full-time, and fifteen were part-time. I received sixteen completed surveys. My survey questions focused on their perceptions of student-veterans' writing performance, whether they had adapted their courses in any way to the presence of student-veterans, and their understanding of the qualities of effective academic writing. (The entire survey appears in appendix B.) I also asked

DOI: 10.7330/9781646421343.c003

respondents several questions about their understanding of the writing veterans do in the military and how military experience might translate to college. The most common answer to the first question was "I don't know"; those who elaborated conjectured that veterans wrote very little. Eight out of sixteen respondents indicated that they had little to no knowledge of how student-veterans might have written in the military.

Out of the eight respondents who indicated that they thought they had some understanding of military writing, most identified basic report-type writing as the principal genre. One faculty member wrote, "From what I understand, most military writing is fact-based and concise in a report format. Analysis is excess." Another wrote that "many of my students were more often told to 'suck it up' rather than express—in writing or in spoken language. If there was writing, it was to be brief/ concise and without elaboration. One student relayed a situation in which he was verbally reprimanded for reporting with too much detail." One faculty member cited a particular veteran who stated that while in the military, "good writing for him was being concise, clear and detailed, and making the information understandable to his audience." These responses are mostly consistent with the research on enlisted service people's writing; however, I should note again that only half of my respondents reported that they had any knowledge of these writing patterns.

As writing teachers, we have developed strategies to meet individual students where they are, regardless of their past experiences. However, a better knowledge of the general types of writing familiar to student-veterans can only help writing teachers facilitate veterans' transition to the academic context.

THE WRITING OF ENLISTED SERVICE MEMBERS

The veterans I spoke with described the writing they did in the service as extremely codified. Logan described his writing in the navy as follows:

> LOGAN: It's very formulaic. Everything's pretty much determined what has to be written. You just change the nouns. And there's nothing creative to it. It's the basics of a sentence. It just gets out the information that needs to be said.

Once a soldier or sailor was promoted, though, the type of writing they did changed. Now they were responsible for "counseling," or evaluating, their subordinates through writing. This writing was much more elaborate and developed, although still subject to particular boundaries. Brian describes the purpose of counseling reports in the army this way:

BRIAN: The idea behind it is to inform the soldier, to go over their career and what they were doing and what they need to work on . . . You want to take a soldier, say, "This is what I see of you. This is what happened. This is what we need to work on. And this is what will help your career in the army." So the idea behind it is to create success in the soldiers.

Mike noted that he spent a great deal of time and thought writing his own self-evaluations and evaluating his subordinates. Writing evaluations also involved collaboration and information from several other coast guard service members, both above and below him.

MIKE: The only challenging writing I ever had was writing awards for people or positive or negative reports or evaluations. To do my own evaluation, it probably takes me about a month. And then to do someone else's evaluation, it takes me probably about two or three weeks. There's pretty much a standard format that they want you to use. It's on a numbering system, like 1 through 7: 1 is bad; 7's the best you can do. And they give you a sheet that has criteria 1 through 7 and how the person documents what they perform is where you put them 1 through 7. And if they give me nothing at all, there's no way I can really mark them accurately, so it's important for them to give me all their information, what they've done in the last six months.

Your supervisor might have a certain writing style that he wants to document, so you kind of know what he's expecting. And kind of when you get to a certain age range, you have your own style and your own way of doing things. And then that evaluation goes up the chain of command. So it goes through four or five other people that all have their own writing styles too. So they kind of add their two cents in there, too.

The veterans I spoke with had developed a variety of ways to read their military audiences to determine the genre conventions of their writing. Sometimes these conventions were made explicit by their superiors. As Brian related, "Some NCOs, they call them, noncommissioned officers or sergeants, they'll lay it out for you step by step: 'This is what I want from you.' Others won't." Certainly, the audience expectations in college differ from those in the military. However, the highly developed awareness of audience and purpose that were exhibited by the veterans with whom I spoke suggests one possible avenue to explore in facilitating their transition to higher education. While it is true that the genre conventions of particular types of writing—counseling reports, for example—were explicitly spelled out, the veterans I spoke with were adept at ferreting out how seriously their superiors took those requirements, as well as additional areas to focus on.

When I asked Mike whether he thought he was a better writer now, post-military, than he was just after high school, he answered, "Oh yeah, by 100 percent." He attributed his improvement to experience writing, much of it gained through his military service. As he noted, "With my writing style, I know I'm a lot better as opposed to if I was right out of high school. I feel more confident, and I've had more experience with writing those evaluations and reports and how to get my ideas together."

The experiences of my interview participants are not unique. For example, Erin Hadlock (2012) surveyed and interviewed nine student-veterans on their histories of writing in the military. Hadlock found three genres that cut across service branches—memoranda, evaluations, and operations orders—that were used frequently and were familiar to service members. Each of these three genres was relatively short, formally organized, and had strict criteria: as she notes in her discussion of evaluations, "the smallest of mistakes could result in a document's return" (46). Interestingly, Hadlock found that "it is a common occurrence for the participants in this study to first deny having done any writing in the military, only to follow with a list of the types of writing they did" (50). I found this as well: my participants would gamely agree to an interview, but caution me that they didn't know what they would talk about, since they had not done any writing in the military. Then they would describe the writing they had actually done in great detail, showing a developed awareness of genre characteristics and audience.

Hadlock also found that the writing her participants did in the military tended to describe or support action—for example, a memorandum was written to change a policy, or an operations order was written to plan an ambush. The strict genre conventions support the action by making the writing easily and quickly understood by those who know the conventions. Clarity and direct language are prized. Enlisted service members also focused more on the content of the writing than sentence-level details and style (although they followed stylistic conventions, or they would have their writing rejected). As Hadlock's participants described, the enlisted service members were the acknowledged authorities on the technical content, but they saw their officers as "knowing 'how to write' (many times defined as correcting grammatical mistakes and polishing the wording)" (2012, 72). As Hadlock points out, this dichotomy fed into enlisted service members recognizing "what the officers were doing as writing and what they were doing as something other than writing that was associated with just doing their jobs" (73).

This finding speaks not only to the writing military personnel do, but to their identities as writers, and it helps shed light on why some may experience difficulty with their transition to college writing: not only is the genre much different, but they do not see themselves as having been skilled writers during their time in service. Accordingly, they may see their task as learning college writing after many years of not writing at all, when in reality, as my research suggests, some of the writing approaches they have learned in the military can translate to college quite well. In later sections of this chapter, I identify specific crossovers between the two writing environments, in addition to offering suggestions for how to talk with student-veterans about these crossovers.

AN ANALYSIS OF EVALUATIONS

By far the most common form of military writing my interviewees mentioned was evaluations—whether of themselves or their subordinates. Accordingly, a closer look at military evaluations may help readers who, like many of the writing faculty at my school, may not have much familiarity with military writing. In this section, I present the ways four different branches of the military evaluate their enlisted servicemen and servicewomen:

- The Marine Corps Fitness Report (FitRep)
- The Air Force Airman Comprehensive Assessment
- The Navy Evaluation Report and Comprehensive Record
- The Army Developmental Counseling Form

These forms serve roughly the same purpose in each branch: to provide feedback for the service member from his or her superior officer. While each form is specific to the service branch, I will be highlighting threads that run between them with a special focus on the type of writing that is required. As I noted earlier in this book, while the specific type of writing student-veterans did in the military will vary based on their rank and duties, it is extremely likely that all student-veterans will have had experience with this sort of writing—reading their own evaluations, certainly, but also writing them for their subordinates if they have been promoted. Because of its ubiquity, the writing of evaluations provides a useful window into military writing for those of us who are not veterans ourselves. In addition to analyzing the actual evaluation forms, I will also draw from ancillary "how-to" materials provided by the service branches as well as independent websites such as ArmyWriter.com, NavyWriter .com, and more. A large number of such websites exist to support writing in the military, and they feature examples of evaluations as well as tips for writing them.

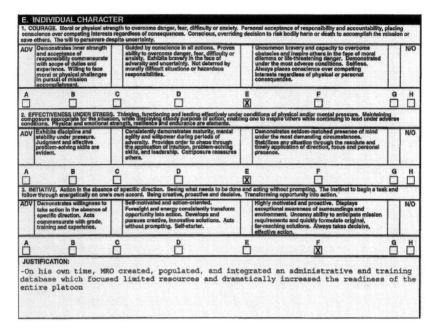

E. INDIVIDUAL CHARACTER

1. COURAGE. Moral or physical strength to overcome danger, fear, difficulty or anxiety. Personal acceptance of responsibility and accountability, placing conscience over competing interests regardless of consequences. Conscious, overriding decision to risk bodily harm or death to accomplish the mission or save others. The will to persevere despite uncertainty.

| ADV | Demonstrates inner strength and acceptance of responsibility commensurate with scope of duties and experience. Willing to face moral or physical challenges in pursuit of mission accomplishment. | | Guided by conscience in all actions. Proven ability to overcome danger, fear, difficulty or anxiety. Exhibits bravery in the face of adversity and uncertainty. Not deterred by morally difficult situations or hazardous responsibilities. | | Uncommon bravery and capacity to overcome obstacles and inspire others in the face of moral dilemma or life-threatening danger. Demonstrated under the most adverse conditions. Selfless. Always places conscience over competing interests regardless of physical or personal consequences. | | N/O |

A	B	C	D	E	F	G	H
☐	☐	☐	☐	☒	☐	☐	☐

2. EFFECTIVENESS UNDER STRESS. Thinking, functioning and leading effectively under conditions of physical and/or mental pressure. Maintaining composure appropriate for the situation, while displaying steady purpose of action, enabling one to inspire others while continuing to lead under adverse conditions. Physical and emotional strength, resilience and endurance are elements.

| ADV | Exhibits discipline and stability under pressure. Judgment and effective problem-solving skills are evident. | | Consistently demonstrates maturity, mental agility and willpower during periods of adversity. Provides order to chaos through the application of intuition, problem-solving skills, and leadership. Composure reassures others. | | Demonstrates seldom-matched presence of mind under the most demanding circumstances. Stabilizes any situation through the resolute and timely application of direction, focus and personal presence. | | N/O |

A	B	C	D	E	F	G	H
☐	☐	☐	☐	☒	☐	☐	☐

3. INITIATIVE. Action in the absence of specific direction. Seeing what needs to be done and acting without prompting. The instinct to begin a task and follow through energetically on one's own accord. Being creative, proactive and decisive. Transforming opportunity into action.

| ADV | Demonstrates willingness to take action in the absence of specific direction. Acts commensurate with grade, training and experience. | | Self-motivated and action-oriented. Foresight and energy consistently transform opportunity into action. Develops and pursues creative, innovative solutions. Acts without prompting. Self-starter. | | Highly motivated and proactive. Displays exceptional awareness of surroundings and environment. Uncanny ability to anticipate mission requirements and quickly formulate original, far-reaching solutions. Always takes decisive, effective action. | | N/O |

A	B	C	D	E	F	G	H
☐	☐	☐	☐	☐	☒	☐	☐

JUSTIFICATION:
-On his own time, MRO created, populated, and integrated an administrative and training database which focused limited resources and dramatically increased the readiness of the entire platoon

Figure 3.1. Section of a marine evaluation form focused on individual character.

The Marine Corps FitRep

In the marine corps, sergeants through major generals receive FitReps, which the corps describes as "the primary tool we use to determine promotion and retention. Few things can harm your professional reputation as a Marine officer faster than a demonstrated lack of concern or proficiency with the Fitrep process" (US Marine Corps, n.d., 2). In its primary guide to writing FitReps, the corps refers to them as "letters of recommendation" that require "a blend of art and science" (4), with the science being the official guidelines for writing them and the art being the training, perceptions, and what writing teachers would term the "voice" or "slant" of the marine. The audience and purpose of the reports are expanded on in detail in the guide, and at the top of the FitRep form itself, marines are instructed that "the completion of this report is one of an officer's most critical responsibilities" (US Marines Corps 2011, 1).

The report has several sections, beginning with information about the marine and her or his position within the organization. Next, the FitRep features sections on billet (job responsibilities), mission accomplishment, individual character, leadership, intellect and wisdom, and fulfillment of evaluation responsibilities. Each of these sections contains space for the

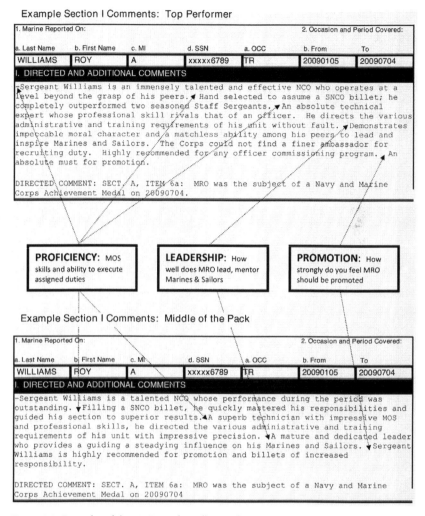

Example Section I Comments: Top Performer

1. Marine Reported On:					2. Occasion and Period Covered:	
a. Last Name	b. First Name	c. MI	d. SSN	a. OCC	b. From	To
WILLIAMS	ROY	A	xxxxx6789	TR	20090105	20090704
I. DIRECTED AND ADDITIONAL COMMENTS						

-Sergeant Williams is an immensely talented and effective NCO who operates at a level beyond the grasp of his peers. Hand selected to assume a SNCO billet; he completely outperformed two seasoned Staff Sergeants. An absolute technical expert whose professional skill rivals that of an officer. He directs the various administrative and training requirements of his unit without fault. Demonstrates impeccable moral character and a matchless ability among his peers to lead and inspire Marines and Sailors. The Corps could not find a finer ambassador for recruiting duty. Highly recommended for any officer commissioning program. An absolute must for promotion.

DIRECTED COMMENT: SECT. A, ITEM 6a: MRO was the subject of a Navy and Marine Corps Achievement Medal on 20090704.

PROFICIENCY: MOS skills and ability to execute assigned duties	**LEADERSHIP:** How well does MRO lead, mentor Marines & Sailors	**PROMOTION:** How strongly do you feel MRO should be promoted

Example Section I Comments: Middle of the Pack

1. Marine Reported On:					2. Occasion and Period Covered:	
a. Last Name	b. First Name	c. MI	d. SSN	a. OCC	b. From	To
WILLIAMS	ROY	A	xxxxx6789	TR	20090105	20090704
I. DIRECTED AND ADDITIONAL COMMENTS						

-Sergeant Williams is a talented NCO whose performance during the period was outstanding. Filling a SNCO billet, he quickly mastered his responsibilities and guided his section to superior results. A superb technician with impressive MOS and professional skills, he directed the various administrative and training requirements of his unit with impressive precision. A mature and dedicated leader who provides a guiding a steadying influence on his Marines and Sailors. Sergeant Williams is highly recommended for promotion and billets of increased responsibility.

DIRECTED COMMENT: SECT. A, ITEM 6a: MRO was the subject of a Navy and Marine Corps Achievement Medal on 20090704

Figure 3.2. Examples of descriptions of excellent and average marines on an evaluation form.

evaluating marine to contextualize the ratings presented through a short paragraph, as can be seen in figure 3.1 (US Marine Corps, n.d., 11).

In addition, the FitRep includes a section for "directed and additional comments," which serves to summarize the marine's performance. The training guide provides examples illustrating how to choose descriptors that indicate the relative performance of the marine in comparison to others of the same rank (US Marine Corps, n.d., 8), as shown in figure 3.2.

For someone outside of the marine community, there may seem to be little difference between the two examples; however, as is stressed

VIII. WHOLE AIRMAN CONCEPT				
1. Air Force Core Values: Consider how well the Airman adopts, internalizes and demonstrates our Air Force Core Values of Integrity First, Service Before Self, and Excellence in All We Do	Airman failed to adhere to the Air Force Core Values *(few Airmen)*	Consistently demonstrated the Air Force Core Values, both on and off duty *(majority of Airmen)*	Embodiment of Integrity, Service Before Self, and Excellence; encouraged others to uphold Air Force Core Values *(some Airmen)*	Airman for others to emulate; personal conduct exudes Air Force Core Values; influential leader who inspired other to embody Core Values *(very few Airmen)*
2. Personal and Professional development: Consider the amount of effort the Airman devoted to improve themselves and their work center/unit through education and involvement	Made little to no effort to complete expected professional and/or personal development *(few Airmen)*	Established goals and progressed to meet those goals for professional and/or personal development *(majority of Airmen)*	Driven Airman; exceeded both professional and personal development goals with positive impact on individual performance or mission accomplishment *(some Airmen)*	Relentlessly pursued personal and professional development of themselves and others; efforts resulted in significant positive impact to unit and/or Air Force *(few Airmen)*
3. Esprit de corps and community relations: Consider how well Airman promotes camaraderie, embraces esprit de corps, and acts as an Air Force ambassador	Made little to no effort to promote esprit de corps or community involvement *(few Airmen)*	Fostered esprit de corps through volunteerism and actively involved in base and community events *(majority of Airmen)*	Active participant; organized and occasionally led team building and community events *(some Airmen)*	Epitomizes an Air Force ambassador; Airman consistently and selflessly led efforts that inspired esprit de corps with significant impact to the mission and community *(few Airmen)*
4. COMMENTS				

Figure 3.3. The "Whole Airman Concept" section on the ACA.

in guides to writing the report, the subtle differences in wording are important to commanding officers, helping them to determine which marines to promote.

The Air Force Airman Comprehensive Assessment

Similarly to the FitRep, the Airman Comprehensive Assessment (ACA) begins with information about the airman, but it differs in that it next contains a section in which the airman is asked to assess him- or herself in the areas of responsibility, accountability, air force culture, and self; this section is intended to "help supervisors/raters understand how their Airmen believe they are performing . . . [which] helps the . . . supervisor tailor the session to an Airman's specific needs" (Air Force Evaluation and Recognition Programs Branch Chief Will Brown, qtd. in Carr 2015). From a writing perspective, the presence of the self-assessment seems to underscore the concept that writing is performed for specific audiences and purposes, rather than being an isolated act devoid of context.

Following the self-assessment section, the ACA features sections on performance, followership/leadership, and one entitled "Whole Airman Concept" (basically, whether the airman embodies the values and comportment expected by the air force). Each of these sections provides space for a short paragraph of comments, as can be seen in figure 3.3.

The *Air Force Instruction 36–2406* (United States Air Force 2015), which provides details on the purpose of the ACA and instructions on filling it out, refers readers to the sections on writing bulleted statements in *The Tongue and Quill* (US Air Force 2004), a style guide for air force writers. *The Tongue and Quill* contains a rich and elaborate section on how to write concise bulleted statements in evaluations, with the overall recommendations being to begin each statement with an action verb (sometimes preceded by an adverb) and to end with the impact. For

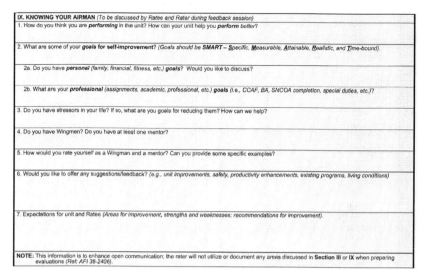

Figure 3.4. The "Knowing Your Airman" section on the ACA.

example: "Processed over 300 records with no errors as part of the 42 ABW Mobility Exercise ensuring all wing personnel met their scheduled clock times" (230). Also in this section, *The Tongue and Quill* provides a revision heuristic, cautioning raters to check their statements for accuracy and specificity and to edit for brevity and impact (231–235).

The ACA concludes with a section meant to be discussed and jointly completed by the rater and ratee called "Knowing Your Airman." This section contains reflective questions, as shown in figure 3.4.

It is important to understand the ACA as a tool for formative mentoring, not summative evaluation: as is noted in *Air Force Instruction 36–2406* (United States Air Force 2015. 2015), the ACA is intended to

> communicate responsibility, accountability, Air Force culture, an Airman's critical role in support of the mission, individual readiness, and performance feedback on expectations regarding duty performance and how well the ratee is meeting those expectations to include information to assist the ratee in achieving success. It is intended to increase Airmen interaction and support at all levels. If done correctly, mentorship will create and sustain a culture of belonging. The ACA is also intended to provide Airmen an opportunity to discuss their personal and professional goals. (95)

As is clearly evident from the "Knowing Your Airman" section, the written document is accompanied by an oral conversation that is intended to be two-sided: while it supports evaluation, the ACA is also meant to inspire in-depth reflection on the part of the ratee and critical

PERFORMANCE TRAITS	1.0* Below Standards	2.0 Pro-gressing	3.0 Meets Standards	4.0 Above Standards	5.0 Greatly Exceeds Standards
33. PROFESSIONAL KNOWLEDGE: Technical knowledge and practical application. NOB ☐	- Marginal knowledge of rating, specialty or job. - Unable to apply knowledge to solve routine problems. - Fails to meet advancement/PQS requirements.	- ☐ ☐	- Strong working knowledge of rating, specialty and job. - Reliably applies knowledge to accomplish tasks. - Meets advancement/PQS requirements on time.	- ☐ ☐	- Recognized expert, sought out by all for technical knowledge. - Uses knowledge to solve complex technical problems. - Meets advancement/PQS requirements early/with distinction. ☐
34. QUALITY OF WORK: Standard of work; value of end product. NOB ☐	- Needs excessive supervision. - Product frequently needs rework. - Wasteful of resources.	- ☐ ☐	- Needs little supervision. - Produces quality work. Few errors and resulting rework. - Uses resources efficiently.	- ☐ ☐	- Needs no supervision. - Always produces exceptional work. No rework required. - Maximizes resources. ☐

Figure 3.5. Definitions of different levels of performance traits on the navy evaluation form.

thought about the airman's goals and performance. Both superior officers and airmen are meant to consider these lofty purposes as they collaborate on the written evaluation.

The Navy Evaluation Report and Comprehensive Record

As is the case with the prior two evaluation forms, the navy form begins with information about the service member and her or his duties. Next, the rater is asked to assess the sailor in a variety of performance areas, including professional knowledge, quality of work, command or organizational climate/equal opportunity, military bearing/character, personal job accomplishment/initiative, teamwork, and leadership, as is seen in figure 3.5.

I was struck by how much these sections resembled a grading rubric; they were quite similar to rubrics I've seen used in writing courses. Following these sections, the form has space for extended written comments (figure 3.6).

Note that raters are asked to provide justifying evidence for low ratings. The navy provides additional guidance for how to write comments on the form:

Space is limited. Avoid preambles and get directly to performance. Do not use puffed-up adjectives. Use direct, factual writing that allows the performance to speak for itself. Bullet style is preferred. Give examples of performance and results. Quantify wherever possible, but do not stress quantity at the expense of quality. Avoid stock comments that make everyone sound alike. Be consistent with the trait marks. Comment on poor performance or misconduct where necessary, but be judicious. Define seldom-used acronyms. Use the sections of the report that have been set-aside for them. Remember the report will be made a part of the member's OMPF [official military personnel file] and that the report is a permanent part of the official record. (Department of the Navy 2015, 7).

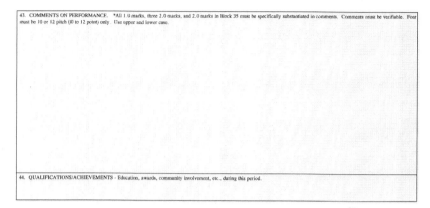

Figure 3.6. An example of a text box for entering a descriptive narrative on the navy evaluation form.

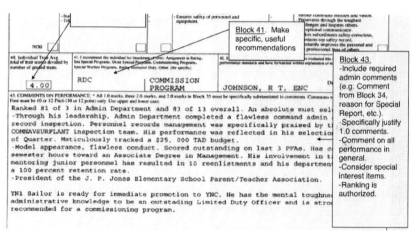

Figure 3.7. An example of a descriptive narrative on the navy evaluation form.

Figure 3.7 shows an example from the same instruction manual (1-35).

Similarly to the army and air force, the navy places a premium on concise, descriptive writing that contains verifiable evidence. The superior officer is asked to make informed judgments about the sailor that contextualize and elaborate on the ratings contained in the preceding sections of the form. Evaluation writers are also cautioned to avoid boilerplate writing, instead personalizing the evaluation by focusing on the specific qualities and accomplishments of the individual sailor. As can be seen from the example, the navy encourages a bullet format, but it does not appear to be as concise as the air force's recommendations.

The Army Developmental Counseling Form

The army defines counseling as "the process used by leaders to review with a subordinate the subordinate's demonstrated performance and potential" (Department of the Army 2006, B-1). While it recommends informal counseling as well, leaders are encouraged to use the Developmental Counseling Form to document formal counseling sessions, which it divides into event counseling (specific instances of performance, crisis, integration, termination, etc.), performance counseling, and professional growth counseling (articulating and helping a soldier achieve specific personal or professional goals).

According to the *Army Leadership* (Department of the Army 2006) document, which provides extensive guidelines for counseling, the counseling document is to be seen as only one aspect of the whole counseling process. In its guidelines, the army covers active listening strategies, appropriate questioning techniques, verbal and nonverbal response, showing empathy, specific counseling approaches, and more (B-4–B-8). The guidelines state that "caring and empathic Army leaders conduct counseling to help subordinates become better team members, maintain or improve performance, and prepare for the future" (B-4). Army leaders are expected to continually work on their own counseling techniques so they can more effectively mentor their subordinates.

The Developmental Counseling Form itself is designed both to help leaders prepare for a formal counseling session and to document that session. As is the case with the other forms discussed in this section, the army's form begins with information about the soldier and leader, followed by space for the leader to provide background information on the reason for the counseling session. This information would be filled out in advance.

Then, the form provides spaces for the leader to document key points of the counseling session, a plan of action for the soldier, and a timeline and method of assessment. These sections should be completed during or soon after the counseling session. Figure 3.8 provides an example of how the form would look when documenting a counseling session with a soldier who had financial problems.

Note that several of these sections—the background information and the first paragraph of the summary—appear to have been written prior to the counseling session: the first paragraph of the summary seems to be meant to be read to the soldier. The rest of the summary, written in the past tense, seems to serve as contextualization of PFC Jones's financial obligations and a record of the session. Figure 3.9 shows the agreed-upon plan of action.

PART II - BACKGROUND INFORMATION

Purpose of Counseling: *(Leader states the reason for the counseling, e.g. Performance/Professional or Event-Oriented counseling and includes the leaders facts and observations prior to the counseling):*

To inform PFC Jones of his responsibility to manage his financial affairs and the potential consequence of poor management. To help PFC Jones develop a plan of action to resolve his financial problems.
Facts: The battery commander received reports from the Enlisted Club that PFC Jones had checks returned for insufficient funds. The Enlisted Club cashier has 2 checks for a total of $200 that were returned by American Bank, NA.
A total of $240 is due to the club system for the amount of the checks and fees.

PART III - SUMMARY OF COUNSELING
Complete this section during or immediately subsequent to counseling.

Key Points of Discussion:
PFC Jones, late payments and bounced checks reflect a lack of responsibility and poor management of financial assets. You should know that passing bad checks is a punishable offence under the UCMJ and local law. The commander has been contacted and has the attention of the battery chain of command. The commander, first sergeant and platoon sergeant have begun to question your ability to manage your personal affairs. I also want to remind you that promotions and awards are based on more than just MOS related duties; Soldiers must act responsibly and professionally in all areas of their lives.

Per conversation with PFC Jones, the following information was obtained:
PFC Jones had cashed the checks to purchase food, pay his phone bill and send money home to assist his grandmother with her heating bills. PFC Jones stated he had miscalculated the amount of money in his checking account and will not be able to cover the checks until he gets paid at the end of April 2006. He also stated that warmer weather will reduce any further need to help with his grandmother's utilities. PFC Jones and I went to Army Community Services and they determined the following:

PFC Jones monthly obligations:
Car payment: $330, Car insurance: $138, Rent and utilities: $400. Other credit cards/accounts: $0 Monthly net pay: $1232.63

We discussed that the remaining $364 should cover PFC Jones monthly living expenses. We also discussed that PFC Jones should start a savings account to draw from in emergencies. Although it is not wrong for him to help his grandmother, he needs to make sure that he is not putting his financial stability in jeopardy. He confirmed he wants to get his finances back on track and begin to put money aside in a savings account to prepare for future needs.

Figure 3.8. An example of a counseling narrative on the army evaluation form.

Plan of Action: *(Outlines actions that the subordinate will do after the counseling session to reach the agreed upon goal(s). The actions must be specific enough to modify or maintain the subordinate's behavior and include a specific time line for implementation and assessment (Part IV below):*

Based on our discussion, PFC Jones will be able to repay the dishonored checks at the Enlisted Club at the end of the month. In the future he will think through his decisions related to his economic needs. PFC Jones has contacted to Enlisted Club and the manager has agreed to give him until 2 May 2006 to redeem the checks. In the future he plans to put money in savings to assist his grandmother if the need arises. His long-term goal is to start a savings account and deposit $50 a month.

PFC Jones is also enrolled in the ACS check cashing and money management classes scheduled for 2 and 9 May 2006.

Assessment Date: 28 July 2006

Figure 3.9. An example of a plan of action documented on the army evaluation form.

While still concise and evidence-based, the writing in this example is much more developed than in any other example we've looked at. However, it is important to note that this example was in response to a specific event and is probably meant to demonstrate thorough and caring leadership. Figure 3.10, an example of a more regular (positive) counseling form, exhibits a bulleted style more similar to prior examples.

PART II - BACKGROUND INFORMATION
Purpose of Counseling: *(Leader states the reason for the counseling, e.g. Performance/Professional or Event-Oriented counseling and includes the leaders facts and observations prior to the counseling):* To discuss duty performance for the period 9 March 2006 to 12 June 2006. To discuss short-range professional growth/plan for next year. Talk about long-range professional growth (2-5 years) goals.

PART III - SUMMARY OF COUNSELING Complete this section during or immediately subsequent to counseling.
Key Points of Discussion: Performance (sustain): - Emphasized safety, knowledge of demolitions, and tactical proficiency on the Platoon Live Fire Exercises. - Took charge of company defense during the last major field training exercise; outstanding integration and use of engineers, heavy weapons, and air defense artillery assets in a combined arms environment. Superb defense preparation and execution. - No dropped white-cycle taskings. - Good job coordinating with the battalion adjutant on legal and personnel issues. - Continue to take care of Soldiers; keep the commander abreast of problems. - Focused on subordinate NCO development; putting the right NCO in the right job. Improve: - Get NCOPDs on the calendar - Hold NCOs to standard on sergeants' time training.

Figure 3.10. An example of how to document job performance on the army evaluation form.

Essentially, then, the Army Developmental Counseling Form is consistent with the forms from the other branches in that it encourages clear, concise, evidence-based writing.

CHARACTERISTICS OF MILITARY EVALUATION WRITING

Each evaluation form reflects the values of its branch of the military, and certainly there are differences in structure and form. However, the similarities that run across the forms shed light on the military writing student-veterans are likely familiar with.

Stylistically, the writing on all these evaluations is direct and concise. It is evidence-based and deals with concrete, verifiable actions. In the guides cited above, writers are urged to get to the point, avoid excessive adjectives and the like, and craft simple or perhaps compound sentences (as opposed to compound complex, etc.). Writers are cautioned to adhere to standard grammatical and mechanical conventions, although sometimes sentence fragments are permissible (as in bulleted lists). Much of the writing is in paragraph form and follows commonly accepted paragraph structure—topic sentences, supporting details, concluding sentences. I am struck by how accurately the eight faculty survey respondents who indicated that they understood military writing (described in the beginning of this chapter) did, in fact, understand it, highlighting its reliance on evidence, concision, and clarity. Yet, as I noted earlier, these eight represented only half of my faculty survey group, suggesting that many faculty at my institution (and probably others) do not share this knowledge.

On a larger level, evaluation writing has a clear audience and purpose, and writers are encouraged to keep those audiences and purposes in mind as they compose. The guides to evaluation writing all emphasize the purposes of the writing and use those purposes to justify the textual features that are encouraged. Furthermore, evaluation writing is seen as important to the overall purposes of the military: evaluations are designed to help the ratee become a better service member and better embody the ethos of her or his particular branch of the military. As I have noted elsewhere in this book, the military is a community of practice in which its members each contribute to the overall mission; by helping service members become better at their jobs, evaluation writers increase the likelihood of success for the overall community. Evaluation writing is seen as important—vital, even—to the success of the organization.

FACULTY PERCEPTIONS OF COLLEGE WRITING

On my faculty survey, in addition to asking what they knew of military writing, I asked them to tell me what they thought was important in college writing. The participants in the survey had a range of experience teaching college writing, from thirty-nine years to just one year. On average, though, they were an experienced group: nine had taught college writing for ten or more years, and another three had taught for five or more years. In other words, 75 percent of my respondents had been teaching college writing for five or more years. When I analyzed their survey responses, several clear patterns emerged, which I have listed below in order of frequency. One will note that many of these mesh well with military writing. Others show that the two communities indeed value some different things in written communication.

Concise and Clear

Eleven faculty respondents argued that a key feature of academic writing is concision, a characteristic also valued by the military. It is likely that the mental picture college faculty have of a concise piece of writing is actually much more developed than what would be counted as "concise" in the military; however, this response demonstrates that the two learning environments share a key emphasis. Following is a sampling of faculty responses:

1. "Concise—waste not the reader's time."

2. "Filter—economy of writing is essential as our society becomes more rapidly paced. The art of good writing is anchored in thrift."

3. "Clarity—so that the message is conveyed as intended. Organization and effective sentence structure: how to achieve clarity."

4. "Clarity—direct sentences that convey meaning without becoming tangled in an idea about what writing is supposed to be."

Highly Organized

The second most common characteristic of good academic writing cited by the survey participants was organization—again, a quality that is also valued in military writing. In particular, one respondent noted that "we rely on similarity of form in order to integrate intellectual data quickly." This is almost an exact match with Hadlock's contention that the strict genre conventions of military writing are necessary to facilitate the rapid comprehension of information and subsequent action. Nine faculty highlighted organization as a key quality of academic writing. Some of their comments are as follows:

1. "On point—purpose and unity to purpose are essential to engagement."

2. "Good quality academic writing contains a strong organizing thesis . . . and a conclusion which circles back to the beginning, giving the reader a sense of expansion, completion, and a way to go forth to explore further."

3. "Organization—be a good host!"

4. "Logical flow of ideas. Effective sentence and paragraph structure."

Strongly Supported

Seven faculty indicated that one of the key components of good academic writing was effective support. Some faculty addressed this in terms of detail and examples; others specifically indicated that academic writing should include research. Some example comments appear below:

1. "Supporting details that back up major points—these are important because it explains ideas and research completely."

2. "Detailed examples. Why? To make a piece informative—easier readability—and interesting."

3. "A premise with good research and written evidence to support the contention."

4. "The prose voice is trenchant and commanding with an authority based on descriptive, personal experience and good, solid references."

5. "Ability to incorporate research into essays."

Error Free

Seven of the faculty also identified grammar and mechanics as central to good academic writing. The term *error* was frequently used, as I mentioned above; however, most faculty respondents also contextualized their discussion of the need for proofreading in terms of audience, noting that readers often are distracted by nonstandard usage or form negative opinions of writers based on their grammatical fluency. Below, I provide a sampling of comments:

1. "Fluid and error free—distractions prevent readers from caring or hearing the message."

2. "Because of my participation in the National Writing Project, I have spent less time focusing on the mechanics of writing—grammar, sentence structure, and style—during first drafts and emphasizing organizing one's thoughts . . . [However,] roadblocks, such as poor grammar, misspellings, weak sentence structure and organization must be eliminated by the final draft. Otherwise, the audience will never understand the message being delivered to them."

3. "Punctuation and grammar—for community college students in particular. Too many CC students are viewed as not being smart enough to attend a four-year college—knowing how to use 'proper' grammar, etc., keeps them from being labeled negatively (reflects professionalism)."

4. "Proofreading—this is how they are and will be judged."

I think it is important to note again how well these four qualities mesh with the examples of evaluation writing examined earlier in this chapter. Evaluations in the military are supposed to be concise, organized, and error free; additionally, the evaluations need to be supported by clear and relevant details. These are all qualities my faculty respondents identified as important in college writing. The situations are different, as are the purposes for the writing and the stakes associated with different pieces. However, it is possible to see how writing faculty could help student-veterans use their experience with military writing as a starting point for understanding how to succeed at college writing.

SUGGESTED INTERVENTIONS

By far, the most important thing to understand about student-veterans is that they are not novices at writing. While the texts they are used to writing—for example, evaluations—are strictly organized and concise, student-veterans are used to carefully selecting words and constructing sentences to get their point across. They are also accustomed to considering the purpose of writing, reading their audiences (usually their superior officers), and adapting their writing to meet community expectations.

Understanding that student-veterans are not novice writers, simply new to academia, has repercussions for us in the classroom. Most important, it reinforces the idea that we should work on helping veterans understand the ways they already write and point out how that knowledge can translate into the academic context. For example, as the faculty survey responses indicate, concision and tight organization are highly valued in many academic disciplines. An understanding of the typical writing student-veterans have done in the military can also point out likely areas with which they will have trouble. One of these is developing an essay effectively and stretching beyond the brevity to which they are accustomed.

Randall Popken's (1996) work with genre and adult learners is also applicable here. Popken studied students who were transitioning from the work world to college after a gap in their educational journey. Like Hinton (2013), Popken (1996) argues that the students in his study consciously and unconsciously draw from the genres they have written and read in their pre-college lives, and that their prior genre experience can help and/or hinder their performance in college writing tasks. Popken suggests that adult returning students are likely to be more successful if they develop a metacognitive awareness of the writing genres they have acquired in the workplace and are able to pick and choose which genre features apply in college writing. This is echoed by Michael Michaud (2011), who writes in his study of adult students that "frequent engagement with a diverse range of genres of writing that encourage the invention and arrangement of extended original prose, combined with the development of deep metacognitive awareness about the differences

Table 3.1. Characteristics of military and academic writing

Important characteristics of military writing (e.g., the military evaluation forms discussed above)	Important characteristics of academic writing (e.g., essays, lab reports, article responses, case study analyses)
Clear and direct sentences	Clear and direct sentences
Concise (no fluff) and focused	Longer, more developed ideas, but still focused—no fluff
Evidence-based, factual	"Evidence" varies by discipline. In a lab report, it may be factual observations of an experiment. In other disciplines, it may be quotes/paraphrases from an article or story.
Clear purpose (e.g., to improve the soldier, to inform others of a situation, to inspire action)	Still must have a clear purpose, although purposes vary widely between disciplines and classes. Common ones are to inform, to argue, to explain, and to analyze. Ask your instructor to help you define it.
Clear audience (e.g., superior officer, subordinate, team members)	Primary audience is commonly the instructor. Sometimes we imagine other audiences—classmates, businesspeople, politicians, attorneys. Ask your instructor who your audience is and how that should shape your writing.

between discursive spheres (like school and work) may go a long way toward helping adult students develop the flexibility and big-picture understanding needed to navigate" their writing challenges in school and work (255). The difficulties Popken and Michaud describe seem to connect with some of the troubles student-veterans experience with academic writing, and it is likely the interventions recommended in the literature on students transitioning to college from the workplace would also be helpful with student-veterans.

Additionally, college writing faculty could do a better job of being more explicit about what they are looking for in college writing. Most textbooks have sample essays for students to use as templates, but many writing teachers develop their own writing assignments or mistakenly view college writing as just "good" writing. We could take a cue from how the military supports the writing of evaluations and make sure to clearly articulate the audience and purpose of our writing assignments in addition to providing fleshed-out examples of how we expect our students' writing to look. This would probably help all of our students adjust to academic writing, not just student-veterans.

For the student-veteran group in particular, though, it might be helpful to share the chart in table 3.1 (or something like it), which springs from the data in this chapter.

Of course, this table is necessarily simplistic. Where I think it could help most, though, is as a starting point for writing instructors to discuss the connects and disconnects between military and academic writing.

Hopefully, this will help student-veterans begin to develop metadiscursive awareness of their prior genre experience; hopefully it will also give them some questions to ask faculty about their writing assignments, demystifying slippery concepts like evidence, purpose, and audience in college writing.

One difficulty that is hard to address, though, is the fact that much of the writing we ask students to do in college is not actually important beyond the context of the individual classroom. I discuss this difficulty in detail in chapter 1, where I compare the learning contexts of the military and college. In the military, even though service members may not relish the work of writing evaluations, they understand the necessity. In college, it is often difficult to discern how writing a given paper matters. To some extent, faculty can help student-veterans make this connection by crafting assignments that are clearly embedded in the work of the academic discipline; we can also more explicitly discuss why we are asking for certain things in our writing assignments. For more on this, I would suggest reading chapter 1.

CONCLUSION

Military and academic writing certainly are different, and I hope it is clear that I am not arguing that they are the same. However, they do not represent two disconnected universes. Rather, military writing can serve as a productive place to build from as student-veterans learn how to write in college. We can help them bridge the two writing contexts by encouraging them to articulate a more explicit understanding of the writing they did in the military, and meet them with more explicit descriptions of how and why we would like them to write in college. I follow up on these ideas in the next chapter.

4

KEY THRESHOLD CONCEPTS FOR STUDENT-VETERANS

A number of other authors have engaged with how student-veterans wrote in the military and how that writing experience helps and hinders their academic writing, and I touch on some of that research later in this chapter. However, to my knowledge, no one has yet viewed student-veterans' writing transitions through the lens of threshold concepts—one of the most exciting and useful new theoretical frames that the field of writing studies has taken up.

In the mid-2000s, Meyer and Land (2005) described threshold concepts as portals of understanding through which learners must pass to truly understand a discipline. Threshold concepts are often troublesome in that they challenge learners' preconceptions and prior experiences, but they are also generative in their ability to pull together relationships between ideas and practices in a discipline and suggest ways for learners to move forward. As Cousin (2006) writes, they can be seen as "jewels of the curriculum" (5): the most important elements of a discipline, the ones that most clearly articulate what disciplinary experts know, what they value, and how they work.

Currently, the key text to address threshold concepts in writing studies is *Naming What We Know*, edited by Adler-Kassner and Wardle (2015). The book represents a "crowd-sourced encyclopedia of threshold concepts of writing studies" (3), a multi-year project that drew its definitions from the expertise of a wide range of writing studies scholars. The book is meant to articulate what we know about writing—what it is for, how it functions, what makes it effective, and how people learn to do it. In this chapter, I argue that the following threshold concepts have special bearing on the question of how to understand and support student-veterans' transition to college writing:

1. Writing is linked to identity.
2. Writing is informed by prior experience.
3. Writing speaks to situations through recognizable forms.

DOI: 10.7330/9781646421343.c004

I expand on each of these concepts below, providing brief summaries drawn from *Naming What We Know.*

Of course, each student-veteran is unique and has had a different military experience (as, indeed, they are having different college experiences). However, patterns exist in how writing is used in the military and in college, and patterns also exist in student-veterans' experiences writing in the two contexts. An awareness of these patterns, coupled with an understanding of several key threshold concepts, can help us anticipate ways student-veterans might struggle with college writing and help us design productive interventions to assist them.

THREE THRESHOLD CONCEPTS

Threshold concepts have implications for teaching and curriculum design, but they also can serve as a theoretical lens through which we can view the process of learning to write. In the case of student-veterans, threshold concepts can highlight key points of potential disconnect between the ways writing is composed and used in the military and in college. Threshold concepts also suggest ways we can help student-veterans build on their military experience to write better in college.

In the subsections below, I expand on the three threshold concepts I think have the most relevance to student-veterans who are transitioning to college writing. I provide a short summary of each concept—in *Naming What We Know,* each definition is written by a scholar in the field—and then use interview data to connect the concept to student-veterans. After presenting all three threshold concepts, I provide sections that suggest productive interventions for writing faculty.

"Writing Is Linked to Identity"

In his description of this concept, Kevin Roozen (2015) notes that we perform and enact identities when we write, highlighting certain aspects that we think will align us with the communities in which we are writing. He also makes the important point that we should understand writing "not simply as a means of learning and using a set of skills, but rather as a means of engaging with the possibilities for selfhood available in a given community" (51). Roozen notes that as we learn how to write in a community, we are, by necessity, also learning what is important in that community, how that community articulates knowledge, and how to participate productively in that community's important conversations and decisions. To write successfully, we need to understand the values of that community and perform identities that are consistent with the community.

In today's all-volunteer military, although the particular reasons for enlistment vary, all service members chose to become members of the military community. Once they enlisted, they were inducted into the particular ethos of their chosen branch of service through training that was designed to transform the recruit into a soldier, marine, airman, and so on—in other words, to introduce each recruit to the "possibilities for selfhood" within that branch of the military. Naphan and Elliott (2015) note that "the military demands that its members de-individuate and work together on tasks" (40), prioritizing the completion of the task over personal inclinations. When service members write during their time in the military, they already "see themselves as participants in a particular community" (Roozen 2015, 51), and while they may need to learn the genres and communicative techniques appropriate to the military, they are likely comfortable with performing an identity consistent with that community.

In contrast, many of the veterans I interviewed had difficulty seeing themselves as part of the college community, and many expressed disdain for nonveteran students. This disconnect with the identity of "college student," at least as many student-veterans perceive it, may make it troublesome to construct a writing identity consistent with the college environment. As Brian said, nonveteran students "don't really necessarily understand the big world and the big picture. I understand how the world works and have a grip on what's appropriate to say or not in front of different people or different groups of people, whereas they might not." Similarly, Ryanne said, "I feel like I'm in a league of my own sometimes, and it's a struggle to relate to people. I didn't have friends for probably four years after I moved up here [to the college town], because I didn't relate to people my own age. I'm, like, the oldest thirty-three-year-old on the planet. I've lived, like, five lives."

In his interview, Logan talked about the irritation he felt at some nonmilitary students who seemed focused on trivial things, and the difficulty he had reconciling that triviality with his knowledge that his military brethren were currently risking their lives.

> LOGAN: I remember I fell behind in my math homework, and I was in the library just plugging away. And these two were behind me sitting there. And she was talking—loudly, so I had to hear it—talking about one of the judges on *The Voice*, and how she wanted to be [like the judge]. I was getting frustrated, because it was such nonsense. I don't want to badmouth somebody's hobbies or what they like. I'm sure she

likes watching *The Voice*. But I couldn't believe how upset I was getting about how stupid the whole conversation was.

For Joseph, the dissonance he often felt working (and writing) with civilian students stemmed not only from differences in age and experience, but also in culture:

> JOSEPH: You know, college writing is kind of an interesting thing in general. You do a lot of group activities in college, and you're expected to kind of openly criticize each other, and then also kind of come together for a resolution or a project like that. And I think one of the biggest things, especially when you're trying to learn how to write in a group, is trying to find some type of mutual ground with your peers. And so that to me was one of the most intimidating parts: when you workshop something at the community college or at the university, and I was going to be four or five years older than everybody else. And I have a different set of experiences and at the same time you're trying to find those common grounds on what you're writing and not bruise each other while you're trying to come to a consensus.

Mike noted that the level of responsibility and preparedness he felt as a college student differed from what he noticed in more traditional-aged students:

> MIKE: It's pretty challenging for me, I guess, because I'm sitting next to these young adults that are eighteen, nineteen, twenty years old or whatever. So it's quite an age range. I think it's just the level of responsibility or maturity. A lot of times, you know, like the assignments are due at a certain time. And like one day this girl came to class and she was like, "Hey, I don't have a pen or a pencil." She was asking the teacher if she could borrow one. And it just kind of frustrated me. I was like, "What are you even doing here?"

If, as Roozen argues, "the difficulties people have with writing are not necessarily due to a lack of intelligence or a diminished level of literacy but rather to whether they can see themselves as participants in a particular community" (2015, 51), the disconnect many veterans feel with the larger student community should give us pause. As Roozen writes, one's writing efficacy is connected with one's ability to craft an identity consistent with a given community. My case studies, especially when coupled with other research (Naphan and Elliott 2015; Persky and Oliver 2010; Wheeler 2012), suggest that student-veterans frequently have difficulties seeing themselves as "college students" in that they may not want to adopt the "possibilities for selfhood" that they see other college students embodying. If success in college writing depends, at least to some extent, on seeing oneself as a participant in the college community and representing that participation through writing, student-veterans' sense of disconnect likely interferes with their success as college writers.

"Writing Is Informed by Prior Experience"

In her definition of this concept, Andrea Lunsford (2015) notes that "even when writing is private or meant for the writer alone, it is shaped by the writer's earlier interactions with writing and with other people and with all the writer has read and learned" (54). Lunsford argues that writers shape emotional and intellectual understandings of writing from these prior interactions, and when we sit down to produce a new piece, these prior understandings serve as filters through which we view the current project. However, Lunsford points out that writers' prior experiences can undermine success in new projects, such as when they attempt to replicate past strategies and genres without fully understanding the new writing situation. In contrast, "when writers can identify how elements of one writing situation are similar to elements of another, their prior knowledge helps them out in analyzing the current rhetorical situation" (55).

In the case of student-veterans, the most immediate prior experience they have had with writing is frequently documents they produced in the military. As I discussed in the preceding chapter, this writing is often strictly constrained, factual, and concise, frequently following templates or models. In contrast, college writing tends to be more developed, and it privileges independent thought and analysis—expectations that can be difficult for veterans to adjust to. Joseph discussed some of these differences in his interview:

> JOSEPH: The biggest thing that I notice is there's a certain amount of free thought and maybe just kind of in general you're expected to expound on ideas [in college writing], when maybe in the military you don't necessarily free-associate with your objective as much. You're essentially just trying to write in an active way to get your objective accomplished or to communicate amongst yourselves. And you're not writing fluffy pieces about feelings or new ideas or "what do you think about this?" You're not critical about things. That doesn't translate necessarily to the academic world. I could see how it would be difficult to force that creativity immediately when you first came into a community college.

Logan indicated that the transition to a more creative, elaborate way of thinking and writing was difficult for him:

> LOGAN: A lot of us have been told how to do things specifically. I know that doesn't sound like there's much room for creativity, but within the military people can get creative when they're told, "You do it this

way." They can figure out how to be creative within a little box. I'm taking a [humanities class], a big freewheeling class. Pretty much, "Do a special project at the end of the semester and impress us." And sometimes it's harder for me now to be creative, when it's like you can do whatever you want overall. It's like if you give me a box, I'll figure out how to make a box really interesting.

John said that when he entered college, he tended to "overthink" his writing assignments: "It took me forever to find out what I wanted to write about. I was having ideas, but I just couldn't get going." One of the things that gave John trouble was that his college writing assignments were much broader than his military writing, and it seems clear that many veterans, similarly to Joseph, Logan, and John, would find the academic community's emphasis on creativity, argumentation, and elaboration an abrupt change from the military's writing environment. As Evans, Pellegrino, and Hoggan (2015) point out, "the process of successfully transitioning [to college] can be hindered by the drastic shift from a role where authority is unchallenged and job descriptions are clear and unwavering, to one where rules are loosely interpreted and followed, and college students are expected act autonomously and be self-directed" (49).

However, not all of the experienced veterans I spoke with said they had difficulty with college writing. Interestingly, both Amy and Ryanne characterized college writing as relatively easy for them, and both described themselves as proficient writers throughout their education. Amy stated, "I've always been really good at English." Ryanne described reading extensively during her downtime in the navy, sometimes as much as a book a day. She also had stories about being one of the top writers in her K-12 education, taking an elective anthropology class in the navy, and helping her friends polish their résumés. These stories contrast with those of the majority of my male participants, many of whom characterized themselves as poor or disengaged writers in their pre-college educations. Of course, my sample size is much too small to make generalizations based on gender, but the question of gender differences in student-veterans' transitions to college writing merits further research.

Corrine Hinton (2013) writes that "student-veterans occupy the same type of liminal space as other adult learners who have acquired expert status in some domain-specific areas but, in starting or returning to college, find themselves in a novice position" (n.p.). She also notes that when her participants were able to "identify and then translate previous learning and rhetorical experiences from the military into academic writing contexts," they reported positive academic writing experiences (n.p.). Hinton's findings highlight the importance of metadiscursive awareness in helping student-veterans transition from the military to academic writing environments. This threshold concept highlights the utility of reminding student-veterans that they do know quite a bit about writing (and its rhetorical nature) from their time in the military, and that encouraging them to examine what they know can help bridge the two rhetorical contexts.

A number of authors have noted that student-veterans' presence greatly enriches class discussions (Lighthall 2012; Street 2014). They often have seen more of the world and its various cultures than traditional students, and they tend to have worked with a great variety of people in many different situations. Encouraging them to draw on these experiences can not only facilitate their own education, but enrich the education of traditional students who sit alongside them. Of course, we often do not know which of the students in our classes are veterans. However, adult learning theory provides productive ways to shape course activities so all learners are valued, not just veterans. A common thread among the research is the admonition to treat adult learners as individuals. As I note elsewhere in this book, Knowles, Holton, and Swanson (2011) point out that the diversity of one's experiences tends to increase with age; similarly, Navarre Cleary (2008) writes that "the diversity of their backgrounds and current life situations means any generalizations about adult students may be even less reliable than those about 'traditional' undergraduates" (114). One way to deal with this diversity is to give adult learners more control over their own learning. Another is to encourage adult students to use their experiences as fodder for writing and discussion; however, we should recognize that encouraging veterans to draw from and analyze their experiences can be both problematic (such as when writing assignments inadvertently touch on traumatic histories) and deeply rewarding, both to the veteran and to the larger school community.

"Writing Speaks to Situations through Recognizable Forms"

As Charles Bazerman (2015) points out in his definition, this concept is predicated on an awareness that we are writing in a particular rhetorical context to a specific audience. Building from that awareness, writers employ genre characteristics that signal membership in a social group and use accepted forms to convey information and suggest action. Bazerman writes that "it is through genre that we recognize the kinds of messages a document may contain, the kind of situation it is part of . . . , the kinds of roles and relations of writers and readers, and the kinds of actions realized in the document" (36). Genres work to speed and clarify communication between members of a group when the group members are not physically in the same space: because the genre characteristics are well known, adhering to them decreases ambiguity and allows writer and reader to act with greater confidence. However, Bazerman writes that if writers

> become embedded in a set of writing practices associated with their profession or career, they may then assume, with little conscious attention to how complex and varied situations, exigencies, motives, and genres may be, that what they learn in that specific context are general rules and models for effective writing . . . Their writing knowledge, knowledge of situations, and sense of genres becomes deeply tacit and less accessible to conscious reflection. However, bringing such things to reflective attention through the concepts of rhetorical situation, genre, and activity systems is a necessary step to understanding their writing and making deeper choices. (37)

Student-veterans have, indeed, been "embedded in a set of writing practices associated with their profession": that of the military. The amount of writing routinely performed by enlisted service members may surprise some, but writing is quite common in the military at all levels (Hadlock 2012; Hadlock and Doe 2014; Hinton 2013). This writing has strict genre characteristics that are in place to facilitate quick and clear communication, and service members learn these characteristics through a combination of direct instruction, models, and supervisor feedback.

Based on my interviews, until they receive a promotion, the principal type of writing enlisted service people do in the military is logs—short, simple records of activities. As Brian described, "They're just real monotonous, like time, date, a short sentence that might not even really be a sentence, just a statement that's not really complete." This description was echoed by Mike: "We constantly do logs, like when we go on watch. You'll have a four-hour watch where you'll be responsible for the engines in the engine room and the machinery running on the boat. So you have to record all that, which is pretty easy and pretty standard."

The longer someone stays in the military, the more likely it is that he or she will write more developed texts. For example, once service members are promoted, they frequently are responsible for "counseling," or evaluating, their subordinates through writing. These reports are quite similar across the branches of the military, and I discussed them in detail in the last chapter. As my participants described, evaluations have strict genre conventions, and even the words can be prescribed.

LOGAN: They actually have a whole book on the types of words you want to use to make somebody look good versus really good or exceptional. It's like a thesaurus that's specifically for writing evaluations in the military. You go through and say, you can use these words if you feel this about this person. If you feel even better, turn to this page and try and use these words. It's kind of like a schematic for fixing a piece of machinery in the military. If this is broken, turn to this page. If this is what's happening, turn to this page. And then pull this circuit card out and put a new one in. It's the same thing with writing.

BRIAN: You have to do counseling statements monthly for soldiers that are under you. I was a sergeant so I'd have a staff sergeant and then a platoon sergeant [above me]. So sometimes the leadership above us would make an outline, like this is what needs to go into your counseling statements. What you did this month, what your team did or what that soldier did that month and then how they performed, their job performance, and then like say future things that are going to happen with the unit or the team or platoon. And then finally what that soldier needs to work on. And then the platoon sergeant and first sergeant would go through all the counseling packets to make sure that they were adequate to standard per se.

John, Amy, and Ryanne learned to do specialized, job-specific writing in the military. John was promoted to an operations chief, responsible for scheduling jobs for around seventy people, and he had to use writing—memos, logs, and the like—to keep track of gear and personnel. Amy was in the Maintenance Management Officers Office and collected maintenance reports from several platoons and "compile[d] them into one large report to give them to our battalion commander every week." Similarly, Ryanne compiled data for the Office of Naval Intelligence, following specific genre constraints for her reports.

All of the student-veterans I interviewed could talk in detail about how they learned the formats and functions of written documents through a combination of templates, models, and feedback from their superiors. They were also accustomed to reading their audiences (usually their superior officers) and adapting their writing to meet audience expectations. One of the clearest threads throughout all the interviews I performed was that every formal piece of writing they produced in the military had a set format with clear constraints. Additionally, although they sometimes rolled their eyes at these constraints, every interviewee could articulate the reasoning behind them—in other words, they understood why the military had put those constraints in place and how the writing functioned in the larger military enterprise. In contrast, they were much less familiar with the audiences, purposes, and social context of college—and, by extension, they were unfamiliar with the genre constraints of college writing.

SUGGESTED INTERVENTIONS

Threshold concepts work very well as theoretical lenses to describe what is important about writing, how we write, and why we might struggle. When applied to student-veterans, they can help us understand why veterans might be experiencing conflict, which is valuable in and of itself. However, threshold concepts are difficult to teach. One reason is that they are so much larger than they first appear—when we tell students that, for example, their writing is impacted by prior experience, this seems obvious to them. It takes quite a bit of thought to understand the larger implications. Threshold concepts are troublesome and transformative, and because they are so big, students proceed through a liminal process of understanding that usually takes time.

In my own writing classes, we discuss a limited list of threshold concepts again and again throughout a course, circling back to them in discussions and connecting them to formal essays. I explain threshold concepts as a whole on the first day of the course, and students read about them in our first assignment. They touch on them in reflections after each essay, and they discuss threshold concepts at length in their final essays. Many students tell me that our focus on threshold concepts helps them understand writing on both a deeper and a broader level than they did prior to the course. However, they also tell me how difficult threshold concepts are—and I agree.

We will not be able to sit down with our student-veterans for a half hour, discuss the threshold concepts I highlight above, and "fix" things for them. Instead, because I believe the three threshold concepts I name above are valuable for all of our student writers to understand, we would probably do well to build them into our writing courses and help all students learn about them—not just the student-veterans. We may also gently and repeatedly remind our student-veterans of them in conferences, or even just ask them questions about writing and living in the military and in college that don't necessarily name the concepts. After all, it is not important (at least to me) that they be able to recite the concepts verbatim, but rather that they understand, for example, how they are presenting a discoursal identity for themselves when they write.

The interventions I recommend in this chapter fall into two categories: those having to do with identity and its performance, and those having to do specifically with metacognition and writing. In reality, these two areas overlap significantly: as the preceding discussion of threshold concepts illustrates, how we write is heavily impacted not only by our prior experiences, but how we see ourselves and how we understand self-hood within a community. Accordingly, one should see the interventions for identity and metacognition as complementary, even though I have separated them here to reflect the threshold concepts presented above.

Interrogate Identity Performance and Community

In the first threshold concept presented in this chapter—writing is linked to identity—Roozen (2015) stresses that we write within communities, and that the writing we produce is, in part, shaped by our understandings of how we fit in those communities. When we attempt to join communities, as we do when we begin college, we present versions of ourselves that we hope will mesh well with those communities. We do this when we write in college, striving to show ourselves to be "college material" by trying to adopt the ways of articulating and supporting ideas that have currency in academia, as David Bartholomae (1986) memorably explored in "Inventing the University." To succeed at college writing, students need to present an identity (or at least a persona) that is consistent with our conceptions of students writing in college.

In studies of post-traditional adult learners, a shift to a student identity seems to promote college success and increased self-esteem in adult learners (Shields 1995). Unfortunately, some researchers have found that adult learners are more likely to self-identify negatively after becoming college students (Taylor and House 2010). Especially among working-class students, identity conflict can be intense: Diane Reay (2002) writes that "they are trying to negotiate a difficult balance between investing in a new improved identity and holding on to a cohesive self that retained an anchor in what had gone before" (403). Reay notes that this can lead to a sense that they are "impostors" in college and that higher education is an uneasy fit (404). Working-class students can feel as though college membership requires them to give up the practices and beliefs of their home cultures, and to some extent, they are right. Reay writes that "if university is too different, too alien, then, the threat of losing oneself . . . is as likely a prospect as finding oneself. The struggle to find oneself implies finding somewhere where one can have a sense of belonging, however tenuous. This is especially problematic for the working-class, mature students who have to negotiate tensions between maintaining a sense of authenticity and desires to fit in" (404). Compounding adult students' identity difficulties is that "stress has generally been found to have a negative influence on GPA and on staying enrolled," and that full-time students tend to earn higher grades and have a greater chance of graduating than do part-time students (Zajacova, Lynch, and Espenshade 2005, 696).

The above findings have high relevance to student-veterans. In addition to qualifying as adult learners who have had a gap in their educational history, many enlisted service members come from working-class backgrounds and have home cultures that are different from Bloom's (1996) "middle-class enterprise" of many first-year writing courses. However, the preceding research should be taken as cautionary rather than deterministic: student-veterans *may* experience some of this conflict, and they may not. As writing teachers, we should be aware of the possibility.

Jones (2013) argues that "those who end their military service are leaving more than just a job; they are leaving a way of looking at themselves in the world, and all that entails, good and bad" (12). The identity shift student-veterans make from service member to college student is addressed in depth in "Crisis of Identity? Veteran, Civilian, Student" (ASHE 2011a), part of an Association for the Study of Higher Education report on veterans in college. The report characterizes life in the military as centering on group allegiance—the individuality of the service member is subsumed by the identity of the group. In contrast, college privileges the individual, and while it has rules, "it also has flexibility and questions regarding adherence to rules are encouraged" (55). College students are expected to chart their own courses and think independently, and academic hierarchies are often intentionally blurred.

The study's authors generate four basic typologies to describe student-veterans:

1. Ambivalent: These students are fully committed neither to their military identity nor to their student identity, and they do not feel in crisis. They tend to be motivated by external factors, and they are at high risk for dropping out of school. They do not have the intrinsic drive that tends to help students succeed at college, and they have not yet bought into higher education.

2. Skeptical: These students "live with a continuing commitment to a military core identity, which serves as their dominant sense of self. The other dimensions of their identity are 'foreclosed,' and in this state, these students experience no crisis and no need to explore other aspects of identity" (ASHE 2011a, 62–63). Such students tend to be focused on "getting through" college, engaging only minimally. They can find elements of college frustrating if they are not seen as immediately relevant—for instance, general education writing courses.

3. Emerging: These students "are not yet committed to change but sense that their military identity, which has been dominant, may not serve effectively in other contexts, particularly in the college environment" (63). This group does sense a crisis as they struggle to find ways to substitute civilian social relationships for military ones and build a new civilian identity. They may feel a sense of culture shock on campus.

4. Fulfilled Civilian Selves: These students have experienced the crisis of moving from military to civilian contexts and arrived at a balanced identity that serves them well in college. This does not mean that they negate their military identities, but that they have found a way to draw from their military experiences while functioning adeptly in the civilian world. The study's authors write that "the various aspects of their identity have balanced out, with the different dimensions appropriately influencing and fluctuating as the environment dictates while maintaining the core identity . . . Cognitively and affectively they have found their own voice" (65).

James Côté and Charles Levine (2002) provide a useful framework for understanding the social dimensions of identity construction and maintenance.

In a late modern society one's inherited characteristics and prior accomplishments often carry little weight in giving one legitimacy in a wide variety of social settings. Instead, people need to strategically guide and control their own actions in order to continually fit themselves into communities of "strangers" by meeting their approval through the creation of the right impressions—the wrong impression management can lead to an immediate loss of legitimacy in certain situations. In late modern societies, therefore, social identities are much more precarious than ever before. As opposed to being a birthright, or a sinecure of social achievement, one's legitimacy can be continually called into question. In order to find a social location to begin with, one often has to convince a community of strangers that one is worthy of their company, and this acceptance can be challenged virtually at any moment . . . The image-oriented identity of late modernity is based on a projection of images that meet the approval of a community, gaining one access so long as the images remain acceptable. (126–127)

Such community alignments are explored at length in Erving Goffman's various works, including *Stigma* (1963), in which he focuses on the difficulties members of stigmatized groups face as they interact with "normal" society. Veterans as a group are not stigmatized in the same way Goffman's subjects are: writing in the early 1960s, Goffman treated the mental health patients, LGBTQ+, and disabled individuals who populate his book with care and understanding all the more remarkable for its time. However, his work has relevance to the current issue because, like Goffman's subjects, student-veterans can feel torn between their military and student identities, particularly when, in the college environment, the more traditional students are viewed as "normal" and student-veterans are "abnormal." As the ASHE report suggests, aspects of the two identities may not be fully compatible, and success in college may entail some amount of letting go of the veteran identity. It certainly entails the adoption of a student identity.

Additionally, a student's fluency in academic discourse influences her grade and signifies her membership in the academic community. Yet new students, especially if they are adult post-traditional students, often have a tenuous grasp on those discoursal moves that signify community membership. In her major work on writing, identity, and adult learners, Roz Ivanič (1998) describes the "discoursal self" as

> the impression—often multiple, sometimes contradictory—which [a writer] consciously or unconsciously conveys of themselves in a particular written text . . . [This impression] is constructed through the discourse characteristics of a text, which relate to values, beliefs and power relations in the social context in which they were written . . . Writers construct a "discoursal self" not out of an infinite range of possibilities, but out of the possibilities for self-hood which are supported by the socio-cultural and institutional context in which they are writing. (25–26)

As Ivanič points out, the roles within academia that are available for students to choose from are slippery. For example, we ask students to claim the "student" role, which Ivanič notes is seen as subordinate and peripheral to the larger academic community in that students are generally seen to produce work that is not of publication quality and does not really contribute to the larger task of academic knowledge making. However, we also ask students to claim the "contributor" role, in which they *act* as though they are full-fledged members of the academic community who design their own research projects, offer innovative interpretations, and build on knowledge.

We ask all students to perform these roles, not just student-veterans. However, as Ivanič argues, the act can be more difficult for adult post-traditional students, who often have a strong sense of their "real selves" that is, at times, at odds with the self they feel they are being forced to portray in their academic writing. Ivanič writes of the students she interviewed that "all of them wanted to associate themselves with some aspects of academic community membership: for example to present themselves as knowledgeable and thoughtful. But many of them felt that the conventions forced them to dismiss other aspects of their identity" (1998, 234). As a result, an analysis of student work revealed "heterogeneous and complex self-representations . . . often jostling alongside each other" (234). As might be imagined, sometimes this jostling was uncomfortable.

Basically, it is important to recognize that when we ask students to follow what we see as the conventions of academic discourse, we are asking for more than simple organization or adherence to a citation style. We are asking students to perform a complex and sometimes uncomfortable set of maneuvers: we want them to analyze the discourse community for key signifiers of membership and then adopt an acceptable written persona that shows them to be a member of that community. Additionally, they need to show themselves to be junior members (open to criticism, still developing) while at the same time exhibiting the promise of eventually developing into full members (contributing to the advancement of knowledge). We seldom acknowledge the degree to which the academic moves we value are situated practices rather than universal characteristics of good writing, nor do we give enough thought to how the discoursal identities we ask them to exhibit might clash with identities they bring to school.

I do not mean to come off as overly grim, just to point out that the adoption of academic discourse is a complicated process. Many students make the transition quite well. For example, in her case studies of undergraduates in academic reading and writing courses, Casanave (2002) found that even though students were not participating in the types of disciplinary communities of more advanced students who had finalized a discipline, "the one-semester experience [of the course] contributed to the beginnings of a shift in the students' views of themselves as emerging participants in academic practices" (78). A central metaphor of Casanave's book is the game: she characterizes academic writing as a series of moves that are bounded by rules and have consequences that are largely predictable. Learning how to write in college is, then, learning how to play the game. Of course, I am greatly reducing the nuance with which Casanave presents her argument; by calling it a game, she does not imply that it is easy or frivolous, or that it is not bound up in questions of identity and authenticity. Yet Casanave is ultimately positive: she thinks that introductory writing courses can give students a head start in learning the rules of the academic game, so to speak, and that many students will eventually develop academic personae with which they are comfortable and that lead to academic success. For that matter, Ivanič (1998) and Prior (1998) are ultimately positive as well. No one is arguing that this transition is unachievable, just that it is complicated and frequently difficult, and that the complexity and difficulty are heightened in adult post-traditional students such as veterans.

If we notice student-veterans struggling with such identity issues, a frank conversation about how organization, motivation, and life experience put them at a distinct advantage in college might be in order. In the back of our heads, we might hold Paul Prior's (1998) suggestions that multiple activities and identities "co-exist, are immanent, in any situation" (24). In other words, student-veterans can adopt the role of student writers without necessarily abandoning their identities as veterans. Finally, although many of us might at first resist this characterization, we should acknowledge (to ourselves as well as student-veterans) that college success depends, at least in part, on "playing the game." Again, one's role in this game does not need to be inauthentic; however, just like other students, student-veterans will need to learn the accepted ways of participating in the college community in order to achieve their educational goals.

In my own classes, I have found that many student-veterans will bring up issues of identity early in the semester, usually in conversations after class. (I have found that many student-veterans seek out a connection with the instructor.) If they articulate discomfort centered on being older than many other students, or if they worry about having been out of formal school for a number of years, I note that I welcome post-traditional students, especially student-veterans. I make a point to tell them (truthfully) that I have found student-veterans to be hard workers who are focused on the course and want to know "the mission"—they want to understand the class and what they need to do to be successful. I also let them know that I welcome their life experience and hope they will connect what they've learned about the world to our discussions and their class journals. I do not have a pat speech I give all student-veterans; instead, I focus on letting them know that they are welcome in my class—and, by extension, the college.

I also encourage student-veterans to articulate their reasons for being in college. The military is a goal-oriented organization, and every service member is expected to understand the community's short-term and long-term goals and work to achieve them. Additionally, each service member is expected to accept feedback from his superior as well as participate in self-analysis to strive to increase his performance. College's focus on individuality and finding one's own academic and professional path can feel isolating and alien to someone coming from the military environment. In addition to asking student-veterans to articulate their goals privately and informally, I have asked students (for class credit) to interview someone currently working in their intended field and discover what the career is like day to day, what schooling one needs for the career, and how reading and writing are used, and to write up the results. For example, many of my veteran students hope to work in law enforcement. Through interviews, they learn that police officers write every day, documenting arrests, traffic stops, accidents, and more. They learn what is important in such reports—for example, detail, chronological order, following the format, appropriate language use—and this knowledge helps them focus their efforts on building relevant skills in their writing. This process also helps them to understand how they fit into the college community, whom they should find as mentors, and what versions of selfhood they can present in their writing.

As my case studies demonstrate, part of the reason student-veterans may feel as though they do not fit in at college is because of their frustration with traditional college students. Most of the time this frustration stems from a sense that traditional students are less mature and have less life experience than student-veterans, and in many cases, this is accurate. However, feeling as though they are a part of college can help student-veterans succeed. Assigning some student-veterans specific roles with class activities—roles that build on leadership skills they may have learned in the military—can help them feel more integrated in the college community. (Stone [2017] also recommends we acknowledge and capitalize on student-veterans' experience with leadership.) For example, I have found that student-veterans make excellent timekeepers in peer-response groups (e.g., they keep the group moving and make sure each paper gets ten minutes of response so they can finish on time). Additionally, student-veterans tend to be willing to speak in class, and they are usually willing to be the designated group member who reports back on a group's activity. It is important to note that all student-veterans are individuals, and that some may not want to be assigned the roles I mentioned; we should certainly respect these wishes. However, I have found that the majority of the veterans I have taught relish additional responsibility.

Finally, as Michelle Navarre Cleary and Kathryn Wozniak (2013) have articulated, student-veterans share a great deal in common with nonveteran adult learners who are transitioning from the workplace to college. I have found that student-veterans respond well to journaling about and discussing readings exploring adult learners. After all, military experience is not the only component of student-veterans' identity; they also are older than traditional students, are sometimes parents, and frequently have jobs or other complicating life factors that are important and exert a pull on them that can make focusing on school challenging. Asking student-veterans to read first-person

accounts and academic studies of adult learners normalizes the dissonance veterans might feel at their own transitions, as well as providing
models of how other adults have transitioned successfully. In my own
classes, I have found that students connect to essays by Michelle Navarre
Cleary (2012), Malcolm X (2017), Deborah Brandt (2017), bell hooks
(2000), and Victor Villanueva (2017), but writing about adult learners
abounds, and rather than focusing on particular authors, I would recommend that instructors simply look for quality, accessible writing that
provocatively portrays post-traditional students' college experiences. It
is helpful to repeatedly encourage veterans to write in journals about
how these readings might reflect their own experiences, or how their
experiences differ.

Support Metacognition and Knowledge Transfer

One of the most important things we can do to support student-veterans'
success in college writing is to encourage them to view their time in the
military not as an educational caesura, but as a valuable step in their literacy journeys. Even though military writing tends to differ from college
writing, an examination of why military writing looks the way it does,
how it functions in the armed forces, and how student-veterans learned
the rules can help them make a successful transition to college writing.

My recommendations in this section center on helping student-
veterans develop metacognitive awareness of how they wrote in the
military and how they will need to write in college so they can explore
the similarities and differences between the two contexts. Transfer
theory divides knowledge transfer into two main pathways: low-road,
which is mostly automatic and deals with simpler aspects of writing such
as mechanics; and high-road, which deals with more difficult, abstract
aspects of writing such as genre, audience, and purpose. As David
Perkins and Gavriel Salomon (1988) write, "High road transfer can
bridge between contexts remote from one another, but it requires the
effort of deliberate abstraction and connection-making and the inge-
nuity to make the abstractions and discover the connections" (26–27).
With respect to student-veterans, Hinton (2013) suggests that "composition instructors should be prepared to explicitly provide opportunities
for veterans to make 'high road' connections between their military
educational, professional, and rhetorical experiences and those they will
acquire as college students" (n.p.).

These suggestions resonate strongly with Yancey, Robertson, and
Taczak's (2014) findings that the development of a personal "theory of

writing" greatly aids students in their efforts to achieve high-road transfer. Such a theory operates, in the authors' words, as a sort of "mental
map" that organizes possible genres, processes, techniques, and possibilities of writing. The development of such a mental map functions
much like a paper map: it allows writers to have agency in consciously
choosing where they want to go and how they will get there. Yancey,
Robertson, and Taczak suggest that writers can develop such a mental
map through repeated and sustained reflection. In their teaching-for-
transfer curriculum, this reflection culminates in a final class project in
which first-year writing students articulate a personal theory of writing.
The authors present empirical evidence suggesting that such a theory
of writing greatly aids students in transferring their writing skills and
knowledge to future contexts.

In journal prompts and formal essay assignments, writing faculty can
guide veterans to explore military and college writing and their own
places in the two communities. Asking student-veterans to discuss how
they wrote in the military, the discourse requirements of that writing,
and how that writing contributed to the military's larger purposes can
help them develop a theory of writing that is quite applicable to the college context. As is the case with all our students, we would like to move
them from a tacit understanding of universal right/wrong rules in writing to an understanding of the contextual nature of right and wrong
ways to write: that the measure of "rightness" is really how well a piece of
writing achieves its purpose within a given context, and that "rules" are
put in place to help writers produce work that more reliably achieves its
purpose. Academic writing also has discourse rules and functions within
a larger context, and starting out by exploring the context of military
writing can lay the groundwork for an exploration of academic writing.

As Wardle (2009) has noted, it can be difficult to identify and
articulate academic writing conventions that hold true across disciplines; however, other authors have made progress in this area.
Theresa Thonney's (2011) study of academic conventions that span
disciplines is helpful reading. Additionally, practicing genre analysis
with student-veterans—and emphasizing the wisdom of genre analysis
whenever one moves to a new writing context—helps them build the
skills needed to analyze and replicate academic writing. We should also
give student-veterans very explicit and direct feedback on their writing.
As Borsari et al. (2017) note, in college, "different departments and
individual professors often vary in their approaches to grading, teaching, and class requirements, whereas instruction and evaluation in the
military tends to be more consistent across settings" (169), a situation

that can be bewildering and frustrating to student-veterans. Because their military experience included direct, frequent feedback, they would likely respond well to such feedback from us (Hadlock and Doe 2014; Hinton 2014; Morrow and Hart 2014). Mallory and Downs (2014) write that "from the opening moments of class, [student-veterans] are inspecting cues amidst syllabi and instructor demeanor, language, and responses to see where they fit and what is expected and allowed" (63). Yet student-veterans should not have to do this work entirely on their own.

As I noted in the previous section, student-veterans share a lot in common with post-traditional adult learners who are transitioning from the workplace to college. I have found that student-veterans relate well to readings that focus on these transitions. In my classes, student-veterans have connected with Tony Mirabelli (2017), James Gee (2017), and Mike Rose (1990), as well as "how-to" articles and YouTube videos that focus on writing for criminal justice and health professions and explicitly discuss how writing in those fields is connected to the needs of the discourse community. The principal goal of this intervention is to help student-veterans understand that successful writing follows context-dependent rules. We want them to understand that they learned those rules in the military; now they need to learn the ones for college.

CONCLUSION

Certainly, this is not a comprehensive list of the ways we can adapt our courses to better serve student-veterans. Nor does it pretend to be a full examination of how threshold concepts might help us understand and support student-veterans' transition to academic writing. However, using threshold concepts as a theoretical lens through which to view student-veterans' transitions to college can help us anticipate some of the difficulties they might have as college writers, and it can help us understand probable reasons for those difficulties. The interventions I suggest mostly center on finding ways to encourage reflection and metacognition to help student-veterans develop identities compatible with college and more conscious understandings of writing.

5

SUPPORTING STUDENT-VETERANS

As I noted in my introduction, chapters 1–4 are designed to be read nonsequentially if the reader so chooses. Each can stand alone in that it explores student-veterans' transitions to college (and academic writing) principally through relatively narrow theoretical lenses—identity construction and community membership; mindset, student success, and retention; textual analysis; and threshold concepts. However, larger themes thread through all of those chapters, and this final chapter highlights those themes and leaves the reader with some global suggestions for supporting student-veterans' success. First, though, a recap of the preceding chapters.

I argued in chapter 1 that even though student-veterans come to college with many strengths, the ways they are accustomed to learning and writing are usually, at least at first, disconnected from the ways we expect college students to learn and write. Because enlisted veterans come from a learning environment that places a heavy emphasis on developing a group identity, and most learning is done in mutually reliant teams, service members learn to count on one another in training and on the battlefield. The military is a community of practice in which all members contribute to the welfare of the organization in a significant way, and the foundations of this contribution are laid in induction ceremonies such as basic training and built upon as service members receive promotions and take responsibility for the training and support of more junior members. Many of the ways the military trains its members are also consistent with andragogical principles: the military acknowledges that it is working with adults, presenting training when it is needed and building on service members' prior experience. Finally, service members' jobs and training require them to read and write, but that writing tends to occur in genres that are highly constrained, direct, and brief.

Much of the difficulty student-veterans experience as they transition to college is due to the differences between the ways the academy approaches learning and what they are used to. Undergraduate

DOI: 10.7330/9781646421343.c005

education is not a community of practice, and unfortunately, it does not tend to provide opportunities for students to contribute in meaningful ways. Additionally, compared to the military, higher education is a solitary environment predicated on individual achievement. Veterans feel that they cannot rely on other students. They often feel that they share little in common with their civilian classmates and are frustrated by them. They miss the sense of identity and purpose that they got in the military, as well as the knowledge that they were vital, contributing members of the community, mutually engaged in an important mission. On a practical level, they oftentimes do not see how the skills they gained in the military can transfer to college, and we in higher education reinforce this sense when we ignore their prior experience and place them in standard first-year student orientation courses and developmental sections.

However, many of the skills and strengths student-veterans developed in the military can help them succeed in college. As I described in chapter 2, these strengths provide a starting point for us to develop ways to better support student-veterans as they connect to college writing. As a group, student-veterans tend to have a strong drive to define and complete "missions," which can be extrapolated to apply to college. Compared to traditional civilian students, student-veterans also have a much more expansive understanding of the world and its citizens. They have had the opportunity to work with a diverse group of men and women drawn from across the United States; sometimes they have also worked with citizens of other countries as well. If they were deployed overseas, student-veterans have also seen parts of the world that many of us never will. Granted, some of their experiences may have been difficult or even traumatic. They were not sightseeing. However, taken as a whole, these experiences can provide a rich trove of ideas and understandings that student-veterans can draw from in their classes. Finally, student-veterans are used to working within a mutually reliant community (something I also discussed in chapter 1). While they frequently see themselves as different from their civilian student peers and have difficulty connecting with them, that does not mean that student-veterans do not have a desire for connection. In fact, they readily seek out connection with faculty, college personnel, and other student-veterans, and they can serve as leaders in collaborative classroom work.

These characteristics connect strongly with scholarship on student success and retention, underscoring the necessity of not viewing student-veterans as if they had a deficit mindset. Instead, we can build on their strengths. For example, a sense of self-efficacy is strongly implicated in student success, and that sense is frequently well developed in student-veterans. Likewise, scholars of student retention have found that increasing students' integration in college communities can lead to a greater likelihood of student success; student-veterans' desire for and comfort with community connection can be built upon to help them see themselves as more integrated members of the college community.

In chapter 3, I focused more tightly on writing, providing an in-depth look at evaluation forms from the marines, air force, navy, and army. I also presented examples of how the military instructs its service members to write in those forms. I discussed survey data focusing on how writing faculty perceived military and college writing and presented interview data on how student-veterans described it. As can be seen from the examples presented in chapter 3, evaluation writing tends to be concise, direct, and evidence-based, with clear purposes and audiences. We can help student-veterans transition to college writing by more clearly addressing the purposes and audiences of college writing as well as discussing how college writing also tends to be direct and evidence-based.

Chapter 4 continued the focus on writing, with a discussion of how threshold concepts might better help us understand how student-veterans learned to approach writing in the military and how we could develop productive interventions to help them understand the college writing environment. Three threshold concepts—writing is linked to identity, writing is informed by prior experience, and writing speaks to situations through recognizable forms—are particularly helpful in understanding student-veterans' writing experiences, strengths, and challenges. Additionally, much of the chapter focuses on helping student-veterans think metacognitively about writing—both that they did in the military and that they're being asked to do in college—in order to develop what Yancey, Robertson, and Taczak (2014) term a "theory of writing" that will help them transfer writing knowledge across contexts.

The strongest threads that knit these chapters together center on community and identity. Each branch of the military has clearly defined roles, traditions, responsibilities, missions, and practices, and those understandings are quite intentionally spelled out for each battalion, fleet, platoon, division, and so on, all the way down to the individual service member. Everyone has a role and a purpose. Service members learned to write in that community, and they understood that their writing—whether it was logs, counseling reports, or more job-specific genres—helped the community operate. Each of the nine student-veterans I interviewed felt at home in their military community and knew their job.

Additionally, each student-veteran knew who she or he was within the military community. As with many service members, all of the student-veterans in my group enlisted in young adulthood, a time of great transition in most people's lives. They learned to be adults in the military. Transitioning to college was jarring for most of them, as it is for many student-veterans, and indeed for many post-traditional adult students who have spent time in the workforce. Andragogy—adult learning theory—has special relevance to student-veterans because it acknowledges that adults approach school differently than children do. To be successful, adult learners need to understand why they are being asked to learn a given body of material or why they are being asked to do a project. In the military, learning is contextualized in the larger mission; this is not always the case in college.

In addition to learning the practices of college, though, student-veterans must also make a transition in how they see and present themselves. As Jones (2013) notes, leaving the military means that student-veterans are "leaving a way of looking at themselves in the world" (12). As I noted in chapter 4, the "Crisis of Identity" (ASHE 2011a) study explores these identity issues in depth and places them squarely at the center of determining student-veterans' success at college. Briefly, the study's authors sketch four general typologies of student-veterans: ambivalent, skeptical, emerging, and fulfilled civilian selves. These typologies can be seen as a continuum of student-veterans' self-integration into the college community, with "fulfilled civilian selves" representing an identity in which they draw from their military experiences while integrating fully into the civilian world. As I pointed out in chapter 4, this is a lot to ask of many veterans, especially if we ask them to do it too quickly. However, student-veterans need to find some way to see and present themselves as "college students" if they are to be successful in academia. Whether we are looking at threshold concepts, student success research, or learning environments, the thread of identity is strongly present.

A key finding, then, is that in order to assist student-veterans in their transition to college and academic writing, we need to demystify the rules of the academic community and help student-veterans feel a part of it. We must acknowledge that for most of them, their participation in that community is transitory, a stop on the path toward a degree and a career. However, the transitory nature of their membership does not lessen the necessity for them to feel welcomed into and connected to that community. As they start to see themselves as college students and begin to feel comfortable moving within the academic sphere, they will be able to take greater control of their own success. If we adopt more andragogical approaches in our classes—ones that recognize that adult learners need to understand why they are being asked to learn or do things—we can help this transition take place. These shifts in our teaching will also benefit other nonmilitary-affiliated students, especially those who are returning to college after time away from formal schooling.

Second, we can help student-veterans understand that their time in the military has value in college. As I discussed in chapters 1–4, military service should not be seen as a caesura in student-veterans' educational journeys. As the veterans in my participant group demonstrated, a great deal of what is taught (and learned) in the military has great relevance to college. Examples include developing a growth mindset, grit, and teamwork. Student-veterans have frequently gained writing-specific knowledge as well, such as how to write clearly, directly, and with purpose. Activities that support metacognition and self-analysis can help make this knowledge portable. Even though college genres differ from military ones, student-veterans certainly are not starting from square one. We can help student-veterans articulate their military learning, make sense of it, and apply it to college.

SUGGESTIONS FOR SUPPORTING TRANSITION

Below, I attempt to highlight threads that appear across chapters 1–4. Readers of the whole book will not find anything revelatory here, but hopefully calling out the strongest trends that surface across the different theoretical perspectives will provide us someplace to start. Although they are focused on student-veterans, most of the suggestions contained in this section—such as clarifying academic norms, incorporating more andragogical principles, including metacognitive activities, and more—would also benefit other college students, especially those who are post-traditional and/or returning to college after time in the workforce. I would urge writing faculty to start with those changes. Additionally, we should keep in mind that colleges are large organizations that tend to resist change (or at least to change slowly), and student-veterans will have to work within those organizations and their norms in order to succeed. In my experience, student-veterans understand this and appreciate being told explicitly what they need to do in order to succeed.

Community and Identity

First, we should discuss academic norms in an open and direct manner. The military codifies forms of address, accepted behaviors, and community norms. The military also has methods of feedback, such as counseling reports, which are designed to help service members understand when they are deviating from those norms and how to rectify the situation.

Although academia certainly has more flexibility and variance than does the military, there are general norms and behaviors that span the community fairly consistently. For example, it is customary to address one's professor as "Professor" or "Doctor [Last Name]"; if a faculty member feels that this is incorrect or would prefer to be addressed in a different way, he will let the students know. It is also customary to raise one's hand in class and wait to be acknowledged before speaking. Again, if this is not the way the faculty member wants the class to function, she will let the students know. When we think about it, many more such norms will present themselves, such as how to contact a professor, how to let someone know you will have to miss class, and so on. Other norms are more disciplinary, but they also can be articulated relatively clearly—for example, what citation format to use in formal papers, how to structure lab reports, and more.

These norms help community members recognize who belongs in that community; they also allow community members to assert their own rights of membership. Mallory and Downs (2014) write that "from the opening moments of class, [student-veterans] are inspecting cues amidst syllabi and instructor demeanor, language, and responses to see where they fit in and what is expected and allowed" (63). Clearly articulating these norms—whether in veteran-specific orientations or individually—can help student-veterans feel as though they understand how college works and that they fit in.

Second, we can encourage student-veterans to connect with the rest of the college community. As I have noted several times in prior chapters, student-veterans tend to have difficulty connecting with their civilian peers. However, they frequently desire connections with college personnel and, especially, with more experienced student-veterans. Even though college is not a true community of practice (as I explored in chapter 1), we can still learn from how communities of practice induct new members. Novice members generally are matched (formally or informally) with more experienced members of the community. This is certainly the case in the military, where new recruits are trained and supervised by experienced service members of higher rank.

In college, we faculty are expert members of the community. We should reach out to student-veterans and help to demystify college. This could be done formally, through orientations featuring faculty panels or mentoring programs, or informally, as student-veterans self-disclose in our courses and we check in with them to see how their college experience is going and see how we can help.

Additionally, novice student-veterans will benefit greatly from being mentored by student-veterans who are more advanced in their academic trajectories (Wheeler 2012). These advanced student-veterans have figured college out. They can help pull the curtain back and show novice student-veterans how college works.

As I mentioned in chapter 4, I have frequently had student-veterans discuss identity issues in my first-year writing classes. I try to make a point of normalizing identity transitions. I do not necessarily use formal language—"identity construction and maintenance" and the like—but we do talk about how college works, and how (as I noted above) communities self-police to some extent by evaluating whether potential members are talking, writing, and acting in ways consistent with community norms. These conversations generally work around to the point that they will want to understand how to show that they belong in college—basically, that they are performing a role (Goffman 1956; Ivanič 1998). This role need not be or feel inauthentic; rather, it is a matter of highlighting certain traits and actions that indicate college membership. Examples might be showing up to class on time, addressing the professor respectfully, asking for help, and so on.

Student-veterans seem to understand this need quite well. Again, I think we should emphasize that we are not urging inauthenticity. Rather, college is akin to taking a new job—one needs to learn how this particular shop operates, the lingo that this business uses. If the job requires a certain dress code, that's how you dress. Writing operates similarly: Susan Katz (1998) notes that "out of all the research that has been conducted on writing in the workplace, one of the most important things we have learned is that every discipline, every organization, and every department within an organization has its own conception of what makes 'good writing'" (109). I have found that contextualizing college like a job reduces anxiety in student-veterans because it draws on something they have experience with and have probably been successful at. It also highlights how one can maintain multiple identities at the same time, since we all tend to be somewhat different at work than we are at home or with various groups of friends. These points ring true for many students, not only student-veterans.

The ASHE (2011a) study I have referred to several times is worthwhile reading. As the typologies suggest, a student-veteran has to have a certain amount of openness to forming a civilian identity in order for her to make a successful transition to college. Also, as the research on identity crisis cited in chapter 1 makes clear, identity transitions can be emotionally charged. Adult learners in particular are prone to experiencing strong anxiety when they transition to school (Navarre Cleary 2012; O'Donnell and Tobbell 2007). We can expect that some student-veterans may struggle to shape a student identity with which they are comfortable, and we should be alert for ways we can help.

Finally, I would be remiss if I did not highlight the possibility that the veterans in our classes might be dealing with one or more disabilities as a result of their service. Although none of the veterans in my case studies disclosed service-related disabilities, I have certainly taught student-veterans who have—anecdotal evidence that is supported by a growing body of research. As Dutra, Eakman, and Schelly (2016) note, student-veterans report higher levels of depression and PTSD than nonveteran students, and Rattray et al. (2019) report that student-veterans with "invisible injuries"—that is, traumatic brain injuries (TBI) or mental health challenges such as PTSD or anxiety—can experience heightened challenges to success in higher education. The Department of Veterans Affairs reports that 11–20 percent of veterans who served in Operations Iraqi Freedom or Enduring Freedom report PTSD stemming from a range of situations, including battlefield trauma or sexual harassment/assault (US Department of Veterans Affairs 2018). In my own practice, I have taught student-veterans who have been injured in their backs, legs, and heads; who have disclosed their struggles with depression, anxiety, and PTSD; who have told me that they struggle with drinking, drugs, or compulsive exercise as a result of their deployment; and who have shared difficulties they have experienced with their significant others related to their military service and its aftermath. I have also taught student-veterans who told me they loved their time in the military and felt completely fine. Frequently, these categories blur—for example, I have taught many veterans who described their service time as the most important and rewarding time of their lives, and yet they were injured physically or emotionally by it as well.

There simply is not one clear and effective way to address these issues, other than trying to be open and understanding to what student-veterans may be going through. I have found that in most cases, if student-veterans require (or simply desire) some sort of accommodation—such as sitting where they can see the classroom's doors and windows, or needing a day off to receive care at the VA—they have let me know. A good veteran liaison can help student-veterans get connected with counseling and learning support services at a college; in the classroom, it may be that the best thing we can do is to be flexible and understanding.

Andragogy, Not Pedagogy

Shifting to a more andragogical approach is also certainly something that would help the majority of our students, not only the student-veterans. However, it seems particularly unjust to have classroom (and college) practices that are set up, albeit mostly implicitly, to treat military veterans as children. College structures such as standardized placement tests and developmental courses that are designed for disengaged or irresponsible students can function, however unintentionally, to send the message to student-veterans that their experience does not matter. As I argue throughout this book, certainly student-veterans may need to brush up their math or writing skills, but they are quite different from eighteen-year-old civilian students who need to learn about time management and responsibility. Colleges should explore ways of giving credit for military learning and, if at all possible, place student-veterans on an individual, personal level (Naphan and Elliott 2015). Many schools have dedicated counselors, liaisons, or advisors who are trained to work with student-veterans; those college personnel should have the authority to place student-veterans in classes that acknowledge not only their prior coursework, but also their work ethic, responsibility, and time-management skills. Colleges should also explore "boot-camp" type classes that are condensed and accelerated to help student-veterans brush up on academic writing skills that they may not have used for several years.

One of the strongest andragogical principles is that adult learners need to understand the rationale for why they need to learn something. As Knowles, Holton, and Swanson (2011) point out, educators do not need to passively wait for adult students to arrive at such a rationale on their own; instead, we can "induce readiness" through such activities as case studies and projects that will demonstrate why that knowledge is important (65). In my own writing courses, I have found that many of my student-veterans are pursuing careers in health (e.g., nursing, paramedics) or criminal justice. These careers demand specific writing skills that can be shared with student-veterans; for example, a local state policeman gave me several templates for police reports to share with my students, and examples of various professional genres can often be found on the internet. Sharing examples of the academic and professional genres student-veterans will be writing in helps them understand the need for, say, precision of language and detail.

Adult learners also need flexibility and freedom. As I noted in my discussion of the military's learning environment in chapter 1, today's military demands critical thinking and decision making from all ranks. Additionally, student-veterans who spent time deployed—especially those deployed to combat zones—have learned to make profoundly important decisions in high-stress situations. We can honor that experience by finding places in our syllabi and assignments to offer flexibility. Obviously, every course has outcomes that must be met; however, it is likely that at least some of those outcomes can be met in a variety of ways. This is frequently the case in writing courses, where we can meet student-veterans' need for flexibility by laying out clear, relatively broad objectives for a writing assignment and encouraging student-veterans to come up with their own ways to meet those objectives (in conversation with us).

That said, student-veterans also need clear "missions" in school and writing courses. While we can and should encourage independent thought and innovation, we need to make sure student-veterans understand what is required in a given assignment and why it is important. A few years ago, I surveyed over thirty writing prompts from faculty across my college, and I found little uniformity (Blaauw-Hara 2014). In a number of cases, it was difficult for me—an experienced writing teacher who is quite comfortable in the academic community—to figure out exactly what students were being asked to write. Naphan and Elliott (2015) point out that "military leaders issue direct and unambiguous orders whereas college course assignments can be vague and open-ended" (41). Increasing the clarity of our expectations for assignments is an intervention suggested by other scholars of student-veterans as well (Borsari et al. 2017; Hadlock and Doe 2014; Mallory and Downs 2014; Morrow and Hart 2014). It is a balancing act, of course, to craft writing prompts that allow for student discovery while being specific enough so that students know what they are being asked to do. However, several veterans I spoke with expressed frustration with assignments that were too broad. As I discussed in chapter 2, a key strength of student-veterans is that they have learned to break larger "missions"—goals—into smaller steps and achieve them. We can harness student-veterans' sense of self-efficacy and ability to achieve goals, but we need to make sure those goals are clear. In other words, we faculty need to understand why we are assigning each piece of writing and be able to communicate our reasons to students.

As I discussed in the preceding chapters, many student-veterans do not immediately see the value of their military experience to the academic enterprise. This is incorrect. The central point of chapter 2 is that student-veterans' military experience can be leveraged to promote success in college. Veteran-specific student orientations can and should help student-veterans make this connection, but individual faculty can, too. We should never put student-veterans on the spot or disclose their veteran status to the class until they do so first. However, if they are comfortable sharing aspects of their military experience in discussions and writing, we should encourage them to do so.

Metacognition and Mindful Abstraction

Many of my suggestions for helping student-veterans develop productive student identities incorporate reflection and self-examination. Adult learning theory also tends to recommend reflective activities to help learners alleviate anxiety and make connections between their workplace knowledge and school. Reflection is also an integral part of transfer theory in that it connects to "high-road transfer," whereby learners mindfully abstract knowledge learned in specific contexts and consider how it might be made portable to other contexts (Perkins and Salomon 1988). Accordingly, I recommend that writing teachers place a premium on reflective writing activities in their classes. Such activities will not only help student-veterans, they will very likely help the rest of their students as well, both traditional and post-traditional.

Reflective writing is usually low-stakes and informal. Frequently, writing teachers will ask students to compose a short reflection on a formal writing assignment, often asking students to describe their writing processes and identify areas in which they struggled or where they thought they succeeded. There is value in these types of reflections in that they help students develop a metacognitive awareness of their writing—they encourage students to articulate what actually happens when they write and grow to see writing as a process over which they have significant control and understanding (Carroll 2002). As I discussed in chapter 4, metacognition and reflection help students develop a theory of writing in the ways discussed by Yancey, Robertson, and Taczak (2014), who found that such a theory of writing can help writers transfer writing knowledge between contexts.

Many transfer-theory scholars also emphasize the utility of "cuing for transfer"—that is, formally encouraging students to think about specific ways past knowledge can help with current projects, and how current knowledge might help in the future (Brent 2011; Perkins and Salomon 1988). This recommendation dovetails well with a common recommendation in student-veteran studies: that veterans need to be encouraged to view the skills and knowledge they gained in the military as valuable in college. I hope that this book has made clear to readers that while not every specific military skill will transfer neatly into the college context, many aspects of the veteran mindset transfer very well. Also, as I focused on in chapters 3 and 4, many student-veterans will have written quite a bit in the military. This was true of all of my research participants. They should not be regarded as novice writers; instead, they should be encouraged to examine what they know about writing and reshape that knowledge in the context of the academy (Hadlock 2012; Hinton 2013).

For example, the student-veterans I interviewed had a strong understanding of counseling reports—their genre conventions, purposes, and audiences. However, they had (understandably) not articulated their knowledge of counseling reports in the terms I just used, which are common to academic writing. This sort of rearticulation is useful in helping student-veterans abstract writing knowledge from the military. Specifically, they knew how to write counseling reports, but through abstracting this awareness, they can understand that they know how to follow a community's strict genre conventions while providing useful feedback to a subordinate. More simply, they learned how to achieve a specific purpose through writing.

Once they understand their military writing in these ways, we can help them develop a framework for success in college writing. Building on the above example, in their other classes, they will have to understand the audiences, purposes, and genre conventions of the writing they are being asked to do. Knowing that they should understand these elements helps them develop a heuristic for approaching writing in their other classes.

These are just a few examples of how we can help student-veterans gain metacognitive awareness of their past and current writing practices. As I suggested in chapter 4, scholarship on workplace writing is worth reading, since student-veterans' transition to academia parallels the transitions of post-traditional students from the workplace to college (Navarre Cleary and Wozniak 2013). This scholarship provides many other suggestions and examples that will be useful as we work with student-veterans.

Before I end this section, I would like to caution writing teachers about what I see as a potentially difficult area that connects to reflection and past experience. While we certainly want to encourage student-veterans to explore their military experience, we want them to do so in safe ways. Marilyn Valentino (2012) notes that not every veteran is a "wounded warrior" (165); however, as Jonathan Shay (2002) points out, many combat veterans do indeed return from war with emotional challenges. While writing has been found to help many traumatized individuals work through difficult emotions (Moran 2013; Pennebaker 1997; Sloan, Feinstein, and Marx 2009), we should really ask ourselves whether a three-hour-a-week college writing class is the best place for such writing. Some personal writing assignments—such as a standard "Describe a significant event"—may force student-veterans to disclose their veteran status to the class and may seem to require them to discuss traumatic events. Even a small modification of the assignment—say, "Identify a significant personality trait you have and describe how you developed it"—gives students more flexibility to avoid topics they find uncomfortable or traumatic while still leading to the kind of self-examination that can support transition.

FINAL THOUGHTS

Student-veterans should not be seen as suffering from some deficiency, but as disconnected from higher education. Understanding this should profoundly influence how we approach their transition. If we approach them expecting a lack, we will ask ourselves how we can fill or fix them; the implicit goal will be to make them more like our vision of the ideal college student.

However, if we approach them from a perspective of disconnect, our questions become more mutual. How can we reach them? How can we help them to reach us? How can we begin to speak each other's language, to understand one another? Connection implies movement on both sides. The goal becomes not to change them, but to change together.

The massive influx of student-veterans is an opportunity for colleges to examine how many of our practices are built around the erroneous assumption that our students are rank novices, not just inexperienced with coursework, but also with life. This assumption is particularly unjust to veterans, who, as I have shown, arrive at college with highly developed senses of responsibility, a polished work ethic, wide-ranging life experiences, a history of successful learning, and practice writing in a variety of genres. These are students who are set up for success, especially if we support them in their journey.

APPENDIX A
Student-Veteran Survey

CONSENT FORM

The goal of this study is to better understand how veterans navigate the challenges of college writing so colleges and faculty can better support student-veterans. I want to be sure you understand some key components of the study:

- Using a combination of a survey and interviews, I will ask you a series of questions that will touch on your history, your experiences in the military, your goals for college and work, and your views about writing. If you would rather not answer a particular question, we can skip it. You do not have to explain why you choose not to answer that question.

- You are free to stop the interview at any time. There will be no repercussions for ending the interview, and you do not have to explain why you want to end it. If you choose to stop the interview, I will not contact you for follow-up interviews. You are welcome to contact me at a later date if you would like to continue the interviews.

- If you are a student, I will not discuss what you say with any of your teachers or with any college personnel; I will not even tell your teachers you are participating in the research. I will store your answers under a pseudonym, which I will also use when I write my research report and if/when I publish my results.

- You may contact me at any time with questions about this research project. [Here I provided my phone number and email.]

If you understand this information and agree to participate in this research, please sign your name on the line below and date it. [Space provided for signature and date.]

Thank you very much for your participation.

SURVEY QUESTIONS

Thank you for agreeing to participate in this research. The questions on this survey are designed to give me a sense of the basics about you,

DOI: 10.7330/9781646421343.c006

your military service, and your goals for college writing (if you are a new student). Some questions are very basic and only require short answers; others are a bit more open-ended. On the latter, the more information you can give me, the better I will be able to understand your experience.

Please do not worry about grammar, complete sentences, etc. I am just interested in the information. You may skip questions you prefer not to answer.

- What is your current age?
- What is your gender?
- How old were you when you enlisted in the military?
- Why did you decide to enlist?
- What branch of the military did you serve in, what was your length of service, and what is your current rank?
- Are you still in the service in some capacity? If so, could you provide details?
- How do you think your military experience shaped your sense of identity? (In other words, do you see yourself any differently now that you have served in the military? If so, how?)
- If you are a current college student, what degree do you hope to achieve? If you are a college graduate, what is your degree?
- Why did you decide to go to college? Do you (or did you) feel like you belong in college? Do you (or did you) have any particular concerns about your likelihood of success?
- If you are a current student, what classes are you taking the upcoming semester that involve writing (if any)? How do you feel about your chances to write successfully in those classes?

INTERVIEW QUESTIONS

Thank you again for agreeing to participate in this research. I'd like to ask you a set of questions about your history, your experience in the military and college, and your experiences with writing.

- Could you describe your academic writing experiences closest to when you enlisted in the military?
- *Possible follow-up*: For example, what types of things did you write in school, what types of writing did you like (if any), and what did you see as the purposes for school writing?
- Can you please describe how you used writing in the military? This could include any training or formal education you received as well as the writing you did during your normal duties.
- *Possible follow-up*: What was valued in that writing? How did you learn what made that writing effective? Why was it important that you followed those criteria?

- Did you ever draw from your military experience during your time in college, either as a source for ideas or for writing skills? If so, can you describe the experience?
- Do you think there are any strengths or challenges that are specific to veterans as they learn college writing?
- *Possible follow-up:* Are there ways colleges or faculty could better support student-veterans as a group as they learn college writing?

APPENDIX B
Writing Faculty Survey

Thank you for agreeing to participate in this survey! My overall goal is to understand student veterans' experiences with college writing so that colleges and faculty can better support them. I'd like to ask you some questions about your views on college writing and your experiences with student-veterans. Your responses are completely anonymous, and no effort will be made to identify who filled out which survey. If you need more room, please feel free to attach an additional sheet of paper.

Your participation is voluntary. If you would like to contact me to speak about this research, please feel free to do so at [email and phone number]. Thank you.

1. What writing courses are you currently teaching?

2. How long have you taught college writing (at any institution)?

3. What do you think are some key qualities of good academic writing? Very briefly, why are they important?

4. Has the knowledge that student-veterans may be in your writing classes influenced your choice of writing prompts, your syllabus, or the structure of your class in any way? If so, how?

5. To your knowledge, have you had student-veterans in your college writing classes?

    If you answered "yes" to #5, please turn the paper over and answer the following questions:

6. What are your overall impressions of student-veterans? (Your answer does not need to be limited to the writing context). How have you developed those impressions?

7. Has a student-veteran ever written about his or her military experience in your class? If so, could you describe an instance (without identifying the student)? How did other students react? How did you respond to the veteran's writing?

8. What is your understanding of the writing student-veterans did during their military service? What do you think might be the main reasons they would write, and what do you think constituted "good writing" in that context?

DOI: 10.7330/9781646421343.c007

9. Do you think there are any connections between the writing students did in the military and the writing they do in college? Are there ways their military writing experience might help or hinder them as they learn to write in college?

10. Do you think there are any strengths or challenges that are specific to veterans as they learn college writing? Are there ways colleges or faculty could better support student-veterans as a group as they learn college writing?

Thanks again for your willingness to participate in this research.

REFERENCES

Adler-Kassner, Linda, and Elizabeth Wardle. 2015. *Naming What We Know: Threshold Concepts of Writing Studies*. Logan: Utah State University Press.

Albright, David Luther, Kate Thomas Hendricks, Justin McDaniel, Kari Lynne Fletcher, Kelli Godfrey, Jessica Bertram, and Caroline Angel. 2019. "When Women Veterans Return: The Role of Postsecondary Education in Transition in Their Civilian Lives." *Journal of American College Health* 67 (5): 479–485.

American Council on Education. 2011. *Promising Practices in Veterans' Education: Outcomes and Recommendations from the Success for Veterans Award Grants.* http://www.acenet.edu/news-room/Pages/ACE-Walmart-Success-for-Veterans-Grants.aspx.

American Council on Education. 2015. "By the Numbers: Undergraduate Student-Veterans." https://www.acenet.edu/the-presidency/columns-and-features/Pages/By-the-Numbers-Undergraduate-Student-Veterans.aspx.

ASHE (Association for the Study of Higher Education). 2011a. "Crisis of Identity? Veteran, Civilian, Student." *Veterans in Higher Education: When Johnny and Jane Come Marching to Campus.* ASHE Higher Education Report 37 (3): 53–65.

ASHE (Association for the Study of Higher Education). 2011b. "Women Warriors: Supporting Female Student Veterans." *Veterans in Higher Education: When Johnny and Jane Come Marching to Campus.* ASHE Higher Education Report 37 (3): 69–80.

Baechtold, Margaret, and Danielle M. De Sawal. 2009. "Meeting the Needs of Women Veterans." *New Directions for Student Services* 126:35–43.

Bartholomae, Donald. 1986. "Inventing the University." *Journal of Basic Writing* 5 (1): 4–23.

Bay, Libby. 1999. "Twists, Turns, and Returns: Returning Adult Students." *Teaching English in the Two-Year College* 26 (3): 305–312.

Bazerman, Charles. 2015. "Writing Speaks to Situations through Recognizable Forms." In *Naming What We Know: Threshold Concepts of Writing Studies*, edited by Linda Adler-Kassner and Elizabeth Wardle, 35–36. Logan: Utah State University Press.

Bean, John, and Shevawn B. Eaton. 2001. "The Psychology Underlying Successful Retention Practices." *Journal of College Student Retention: Research, Theory & Practice* 3 (1): 73–89.

Blaauw-Hara, Mark. 2014. "Transfer Theory, Threshold Concepts, and First-Year Composition: Connecting Writing Courses to the Rest of the College." *Teaching English in the Two-Year College* 41 (4): 354–365.

Blakeslee, Ann, and Cathy Fleischer. 2010. *Becoming a Writing Researcher*. Mahwah, NJ: Taylor & Francis.

Bloom, Lynn Z. 1996. "Freshman Composition as a Middle-Class Enterprise." *College English* 58 (6): 654–675.

Borsari, Brian, Ali Yurasek, Mary Beth Miller, James G. Murphy, Meghan E. McDevitt-Murphy, Matthew P. Martens, Monica G. Darcy, and Kate B. Carey. 2017. "Student Service Members/Veterans on Campus: Challenges for Reintegration." *American Journal of Orthopsychiatry* 87 (2): 166–175.

Brandt, Deborah. 2017. "Sponsors of Literacy." In *Writing about Writing: A College Reader*, edited by Elizabeth Wardle and Doug Downs, 68–99. Boston: Bedford/St. Martin's.

Brent, Doug. 2011. "Transfer, Transformation, and Rhetorical Knowledge: Insights from Transfer Theory." *Journal of Business and Technical Communication* 25:396–419.

DOI: 10.7330/9781646421343.c008

Bryan, Craig J., and AnnaBelle O. Bryan. 2015. "Sociodemographic Correlates of Suicidal Thoughts and Behaviors among College Student Service Members/Veterans." *Journal of American College Health* 63 (7): 502–507.

Burgess, Amy, and Roz Ivanič. 2010. "Writing and Being Written: Issues of Identity across Timescales." *Written Communication* 27:228–255.

Campbell, Robyn, and Shelley A. Riggs. 2015. "The Role of Psychological Symptomatology and Social Support in the Academic Adjustment of Previously Deployed Student Veterans." *Journal of American College Health* 63 (7): 473–481.

Carr, Jette. 2015. "How To: The Airman Comprehensive Assessment." US Air Force. https://www.af.mil/news/article-display/article/580200/how-to-the-airman-comprehensive-assessment/.

Carroll, Lee Ann. 2002. *Rehearsing New Roles: How College Students Develop as Writers*. Carbondale: Southern Illinois University Press.

Casanave, Christine Pearson. 2002. *Writing Games: Multicultural Case Studies of Academic Literacy Practices in Higher Education*. Mahwah, NJ: Earlbaum.

Charmaz, Kathy. 2006. *Constructing Grounded Theory: A Practical Guide through Qualitative Analysis*. Thousand Oaks, CA: Sage.

Cheney, Ann M., Audrey Dunn, Brenda M. Booth, Libby Frith, and Geoffrey M. Curran. 2013. "The Intersections of Gender and Power in Women Veterans' Experiences of Substance Use and VA Care." *Annals of Anthropological Practice* 37 (2): 149–171.

Close, Wendy, and Scott Solberg. 2008. "Predicting Achievement, Distress, and Retention among Lower-Income Latino Youth." *Journal of Vocational Behavior* 72 (1): 31–42.

Cornell-d'Echert, Blaise. 2012. "Beyond Training: New Ideas for Military Forces Operating beyond War." *New Directions for Adult & Continuing Education* 136:17–27.

Côté, James E., and Charles G. Levine. 2002. *Identity Formation, Agency, and Culture: A Social Psychological Synthesis*. Mahwah, NJ: Erlbaum.

Cousin, Glynis. 2002. "An Introduction to Threshold Concepts." *Planet* 17:4–5.

Crede, Erin, Maura Borrego, and Lisa D. McNair. 2010. "Application of Community of Practice Theory to the Preparation of Engineering Graduate Students for Faculty Careers." *Advances in Engineering Education* 2 (2): 1–22.

Creswell, John. 2012. *Educational Research: Planning, Conducting, and Evaluating Quantitative and Qualitative Research*. Boston: Pearson.

Dannels, Deanna P. 2000. "Learning to Be Professional: Technical Classroom Discourse, Practice, and Professional Identity Construction." *Journal of Business and Technical Communication* 14 (1): 5–37.

Deil-Amen, Regina. 2011. "Socio-Integrative Moments: Rethinking Academic and Social Integration among Two-Year College Students in Career-Related Programs." *Journal of Higher Education* 82 (1): 54–91.

Department of the Army. 2006. *Army Leadership: Competent, Confident, and Agile*. https://www.armywriter.com/fm6-22.pdf.

Department of the Navy. 2015. *Bupers Instruction 1610.10D*. https://www.mcmilitarylaw.com/documents/1610.10d.pdf.

Dever, Mary. 2019. "With Historic Number of Women in Uniform, the Vet Community Is about to Change." Military.com. https://www.military.com/daily-news/2019/03/11/historic-number-women-uniform-vet-community-about-change.html.

Diramio, David, Kathryn Jarvis, Susan Iverson, Christin Seher, and Rachel Anderson. 2015. "Out from the Shadows: Female Student Veterans and Help-Seeking." *College Student Journal* 49 (1): 49–68.

Doe, Sue, and William W. Doe. 2013. "Residence Time and Military Workplace Literacies." *Composition Forum* 28. https://compositionforum.com/issue/28/residence-time.php.

Doe, Sue, and Lisa Langstraat, eds. 2014. *Generation Vet: Composition, Student-Veterans, and the Post-9/11 University*. Logan: Utah State University Press.

Downs, Doug, and Elizabeth Wardle. 2007. "Teaching about Writing, Righting Misconceptions: (Re)envisioning 'First-Year Composition' as 'Introduction to Writing Studies.'" *College Composition and Communication* 58 (4): 552–584.

Dutra, Samantha T., Aaron M. Eakman, and Catherine L. Schelly. 2016. "Psychosocial Characteristics of Student Veterans with Service-Related Disabilities: Implications for Further Research and Occupational Therapy Involvement." *Occupational Therapy in Mental Health* 32 (2): 146–166.

Elliott, Marta. 2014. "Predicting Problems on Campus: An Analysis of College Student Veterans." *Analyses of Social Issues and Public Policy* 15 (1): 105–126.

Evans, John J., Lauren Pellegrino, and Chad Hoggan. 2015. "Supporting Veterans at the Community College: A Review of the Literature." *Community College Enterprise* 21 (1): 47–65.

Fearon, Colm, Heather McLaughlin, and Tan Yoke Eng. 2012. "Using Student Group Work in Higher Education to Emulate Professional Communities of Practice." *Education + Training* 54 (2–3): 114–125.

Fontana, Andrea, and James H. Frey. 1998. "Interviewing: The Art of Science." In *Strategies of Qualitative Inquiry*, edited by Norman K. Denzin and Yvonna S. Lincoln, 47–78. Thousand Oaks, CA: Sage.

Gann, Sarah. M. 2012. "'There Is a Lot of Self-Reliance': Modern Military Veterans and the Challenge of Effective Transition from Soldier to Student." *Journal of Military Experience* 2 (1): 211–228.

Gee, James Paul. 2017. "Literacy, Discourse, and Linguistics: Introduction." In *Writing about Writing: A College Reader*, edited by Elizabeth Wardle and Doug Downs, 274–295. Boston: Bedford/St. Martin's.

Glesne, Corrine, and Alan Peshkin. 1992. *Becoming Qualitative Researchers: An Introduction.* White Plains, NY: Longman.

Goffman, Erving. 1956. *The Presentation of Self in Everyday Life.* New York: Anchor.

Goffman, Erving. 1963. *Stigma: Notes on the Management of Spoiled Identity.* New York: Simon & Schuster.

Hadlock, Erin D. 2012. "The Role of Genre, Identity, and Rhetorical Agency in the Military Writings of Post-9/11 Student-Veterans." MA thesis, Colorado State University.

Hadlock, Erin, and Sue Doe. 2014. "Not Just 'Yes Sir, No Sir': How Genre and Agency Interact in Student-Veteran Writing." In *Generation Vet: Composition, Student-Veterans, and the Post-9/11 University*, edited by Sue Doe and Lisa Langstraat, 73–94. Logan: Utah State University Press.

Hart, Alexis D., and Roger Thompson. 2013. *"An Ethical Obligation": Promising Practices for Student-Veterans in College Writing Classrooms.* http://www.ncte.org/library/NCTEFiles/Groups/CCCC/AnEthicalObligation.pdf.

Hart, Alexis D., and Roger Thompson. 2016. "Veterans in the Writing Classroom: Three Programmatic Approaches to Facilitate the Transition from the Military to Higher Education." *College Composition and Communication* 68 (2): 345–371.

Heineman, Judie A. 2017. "From Boots to Suits: Women Veterans Transitioning to Community College Students." *New Directions for Community Colleges* 2017 (179): 77–88.

Herrington, Anne J., and Marcia Curtis. 2000. *Persons in Process: Four Stories of Writing and Personal Development in College.* Urbana, IL: NCTE.

Hinton, Corrine E. 2013. "'The Military Taught Me Something about Writing': How Student Veterans Complicate the Novice-to-Expert Continuum in First-Year Composition." *Composition Forum* 28. http://compositionforum.com/issue/28/novice-to-expert.php.

Hinton, Corrine E. 2014. "'Front and Center': Marine Student-Veterans, Collaboration, and the Writing Center." In *Generation Vet: Composition, Student-Veterans, and the Post-9/11 University*, edited by Sue Doe and Lisa Langstraat, 257–281. Logan: Utah State University Press.

hooks, bell. 2000. *Where We Stand: Class Matters.* New York: Routledge.

Huynh-Hohnbaum, Anh-Luu T., JoAnn Damron-Rodriguez, Donna L. Washington, Valentine Villa, and Nancy Harada. 2003. "Exploring the Diversity of Women Veterans' Identity to Improve the Delivery of Veterans' Health Services." *Journal of Women & Social Work* 18 (2): 165–176.

Ivanič, Roz. 1998. *Writing and Identity: The Discoursal Construction of Identity in Academic Writing.* Philadelphia: John Benjamins.

Jenner, Brandy M. 2017. "Student Veterans and the Transition to Higher Education: Integrating Existing Literatures." *Journal of Veterans Studies* 2 (2): 26–44.

Jones, Kevin C. 2013. "Understanding Student Veterans in Transition." *Qualitative Report* 18 (74): 1–14.

Katz, Susan M. 1998. "Part I—Learning to Write in Organizations: What Newcomers Learn about Writing on the Job." *IEEE Transactions on Professional Communication* 41 (2): 107–115.

Keast, Darren. 2013. "A Class for Vets, Not by a Vet: Developing a Veteran-Friendly Composition Course at City College of San Francisco." *Composition Forum* 28. http://compositionforum.com/issue/28/class-for-vets.php.

Knowles, Malcolm. S., Elwood F. Holton, and Richard A. Swanson. 2011. *The Adult Learner.* 7th ed. New York: Taylor & Francis.

Lave, Jean, and Etienne Wenger. 1991. *Situated Learning: Legitimate Peripheral Participation.* Cambridge: Cambridge University Press.

LeCourt, Donna. 2006. "Performing Working-Class Identity in Composition: Toward a Pedagogy of Textual Practice." *College English* 69 (1): 30–51.

Lighthall, Alison. 2012. "Ten Things You Should Know about Today's Student Veteran." *Thought & Action* 28:81–90.

Lillis, Theresa M. 2001. *Student Writing: Access, Regulation, Desire.* New York: Routledge.

Lunsford, Andrea. 2015. "Writing Is Informed by Prior Experience." In *Naming What We Know: Threshold Concepts of Writing Studies*, edited by Linda Adler-Kassner and Elizabeth Wardle, 54. Logan: Utah State University Press.

Mallory, Angie, and Doug Downs. 2014. "Uniform Meets Rhetoric: Excellence through Interaction." In *Generation Vet: Composition, Student-Veterans, and the Post-9/11 University*, edited by Sue Doe and Lisa Langstraat, 51–72. Logan: Utah State University Press.

Martin, Travis L. 2012. "Combat in the Classroom." *Writing on the Edge* 22 (1): 27–35.

McBain, Lesley, Young M. Kim, Bryan J. Cook, and Kathy M. Snead. 2012. "From Soldier to Student II: Assessing Campus Programs for Veterans and Service Members." American Council on Education. https://www.acenet.edu/news-room/Documents/From-Soldier-to-Student-II-Assessing-Campus-Programs.pdf.

McGivney, Veronica. 2004. "Understanding Persistence in Adult Learning." *Open Learning* 19 (1): 33–46.

Mertes, Scott J., and Richard E. Hoover. 2014. "Predictors of First-Year Retention in a Community College." *Community College Journal of Research and Practice* 38 (7): 651–660.

Meyer, Jan H. F., and Ray Land. 2005. "Threshold Concepts and Troublesome Knowledge (2): Epistemological Considerations and a Conceptual Framework for Teaching and Learning." *Higher Education* 49:373–388.

Michaud, Michael J. 2011. "The 'Reverse Commute': Adult Students and the Transition from Professional to Academic Literacy." *Teaching English in the Two-Year College* 38 (3): 244–257.

Military Friendly. 2018. "Military Friendly." http://militaryfriendly.com/.

Mirabelli, Tony. 2017. "Learning to Serve: The Language and Literacy of Food Service Workers." In *Writing about Writing: A College Reader*, edited by Elizabeth Wardle and Doug Downs, 298–317. Boston: Bedford/St. Martin's.

Moran, Molly Hurley. 2013. "Writing and Healing from Trauma: An Interview with James Pennebaker." *Composition Forum* 28. https://compositionforum.com/issue/28/pennebaker.php.

Morrow, Sean, and Alexis Hart. 2014. "Veterans in College Writing Classes: Understanding and Embracing the Mutual Benefit." In *Generation Vet: Composition, Student-Veterans, and the Post-9/11 University*, edited by Sue Doe and Lisa Langstraat, 31–50. Logan: Utah State University Press.

Morton, Janne. 2012. "Communities of Practice in Higher Education: A Challenge from the Discipline of Architecture." *Linguistics and Education* 23:100–111.

Naphan, Dara E., and Marta Elliott. 2015. "Role Exit from the Military: Student Veterans' Perceptions of Transitioning from the U.S. Military to Higher Education." *Qualitative Report* 20 (2): 36–48.

Navarre Cleary, Michelle. 2008. "What WPAs Need to Know to Prepare New Teachers to Work with Adult Students." *WPA: Writing Program Administration* 32 (1): 113–128.

Navarre Cleary, Michelle. 2012. "Anxiety and the Newly Returned Adult Student." *Teaching English in the Two-Year College* 39 (4): 364–376.

Navarre Cleary, Michelle, and Kathryn Wozniak. 2013. "Veterans as Adult Learners in Composition Courses." *Composition Forum* 28. http://compositionforum.com/issue/28/adult-learners.php.

O'Donnell, Victoria L., and Jane Tobbell. 2007. "The Transition of Adult Students to Higher Education: Legitimate Peripheral Participation in a Community of Practice?" *Adult Education Quarterly* 57 (4): 312–328.

O'Neill, Susan, and Margareta M. Thompson. 2013. "Supporting Academic Persistence in Low-Skilled Adult Learners." *Support for Learning* 28 (4): 162–172.

Pennebaker, James W. 1997. "Writing about Emotional Experiences as a Therapeutic Process." *Psychological Science* 8 (3): 162–166.

Perkins, David N., and Gavriel Salomon. 1988. "Teaching for Transfer." *Educational Leadership* 46 (1): 22–32.

Perkins-Gough, Deborah. 2013. "The Significance of Grit: A Conversation with Angela Lee Duckworth." *Educational Leadership* 71 (1): 14–20.

Persky, Karen, and Diane Oliver. 2010. "Veterans Coming Home to the Community College: Linking Research and Practice." *Community College Journal of Research and Practice* 35 (1–2): 111–120.

Persyn, John M., and Cheryl J. Polson. 2012. "Evolution and Influence of Military Adult Education." *New Directions for Adult and Continuing Education* 136:5–16.

Popken, Randall. 1996. "A Study of the Genre Repertoires of Adult Writers." *Writing Instructor* 15:85–93.

Prior, Paul A. 1998. *Writing/Disciplinarity: A Sociohistoric Account of Literate Activity in the Academy*. Mahway, NJ: Earlbaum.

Radford, Alexandra W. 2011. "Military Service Members and Veterans: A Profile of Those Enrolled in Undergraduate and Graduate Education in 2007–08." *Stats in Brief*. US Department of Education. http://nces.ed.gov/pubs2011/2011163.pdf.

Rattray, Nicholas A., Diana M. Natividad, Richard M. Frankel, Gala True, Michelle P. Salyers, and Marina Kukla. 2019. "The Long and Winding Road to Postsecondary Education for U.S. Veterans with Invisible Injuries." *Psychiatric Rehabilitation Journal* 42 (3): 284–295.

Reay, Diane. 2002. "Class, Authenticity, and the Transition to Higher Education for Mature Students." *Sociological Review* 50:398–418.

Roozen, Kevin. 2015. "Writing Is Linked to Identity." In *Naming What We Know: Threshold Concepts of Writing Studies*, edited by Linda Adler-Kassner and Elizabeth Wardle, 50–51. Logan: Utah State University Press.

Rose, Mike. 1990. *Lives on the Boundary*. New York: Penguin.

Rumann, Corey B., and Florence A. Hamrick. 2010. "Student Veterans in Transition: Re-enrolling After War Zone Deployment." *Journal of Higher Education* 81 (4): 431–458.

Rumann, Corey, Marisa Rivera, and Ignacio Hernandez. 2011. "Student Veterans and Community Colleges." *New Directions for Community Colleges* 155:51–58.

Sander, Libby. 2012. "With GI Bill's Billions at Stake, Colleges Compete to Lure Veterans." *Chronicle of Higher Education*, May 4. https://www.chronicle.com/article/with-gi-bills-billions-at-stake-colleges-compete-to-lure-veterans/.

Saunders, Carolyn E. 1991. "Pedagogy vs. Andragogy: Are We Treating Our Students Like Children?" *Military Intelligence* 17 (1): 42.

Schell, Eileen E., and Ivy Kleinbart. 2014 "'I Have to Speak Out': Writing with Veterans in a Community Writing Group." In *Generation Vet: Composition, Student-Veterans, and the Post-9/11 University*, edited by Sue Doe and Lisa Langstraat, 119–139. Logan: Utah State University Press.

Shay, Jonathan. 2002. *Odysseus in America*. New York: Scribner.

Shields, Nancy. 1995. "The Link between Student Identity, Attributions, and Self-Esteem among Adult, Returning Students." *Sociological Perspectives* 38 (2): 261–272.

Sloan, Denise M., Brian A. Feinstein, and Brian P. Marx. 2009. "The Durability of Beneficial Health Effects Associated with Expressive Writing." *Anxiety, Stress, & Coping* 22 (5): 509–523.

Stake, Robert E. 1995. *The Art of Case-Study Research*. Thousand Oaks, CA: Sage.

Stake, Robert E. 1998. "Case Studies." In *Strategies of Qualitative Inquiry*, edited by Norman K. Denzin and Yvonna S. Lincoln, 86–109. Thousand Oaks, CA: Sage.

Stone, Sharon L. M. 2017. "Internal Voices, External Constraints: Exploring the Impact of Military Service on Student Development." *Journal of College Student Development* 58 (3): 365–384.

Street, Mark. 2014. "Military Veterans Bring Value to the Classroom." *Chronicle of Higher Education*, April 21. http://chronicle.com/article/Military-Veterans-Bring-Value/146113.

Stuart, G. Rob, Cecilia Rios-Aguilar, and Regina Deil-Amen. 2014. "'How Much Economic Value Does My Credential Have?' Reformulating Tinto's Model to Study Students' Persistence in Community Colleges." *Community College Review* 42 (4): 327–341.

Taylor, Jacqui, and Becky House. 2010. "An Exploration of Identity, Motivations and Concerns of Nontraditional Students at Different Stages of Higher Education." *Psychology Teaching Review* 16 (1): 46–54.

Thompson, Roger. 2014. "Recognizing Silence: Composition, Writing, and the Ethical Space for War." In *Generation Vet: Composition, Student-Veterans, and the Post-9/11 University*, edited by Sue Doe and Lisa Langstraat, 199–215. Logan: Utah State University Press.

Thonney, Teresa. 2011. "Teaching the Conventions of Academic Discourse." *Teaching English in the Two-Year College* 38 (4): 347–362.

Tinto, Vincent. 1987. *Leaving College: Rethinking the Causes and Cures of Student Attrition*, 2nd ed. Chicago: University of Chicago Press.

Trainee Guide for Navy Pride and Professionalism Workshop. 2008. General Dynamics Information Technology. https://www.yumpu.com/en/document/read/3888909/trainee-guide-for-cnic-the-us-navy.

Trobaugh, Elizabeth M. 2018. "Women, Regardless: Understanding Gender Bias in U.S. Military Integration." *Joint Force Quarterly* 88. https://ndupress.ndu.edu/Publications/Article/1411860/women-regardless-understanding-gender-bias-in-us-military-integration/.

US Air Force. 2004. *The Tongue and Quill*. https://www.marines.mil/portals/1/Publications/AFH%2033-337.pdf?ver=2012-10-11-163148-597.

US Air Force. 2015. *Air Force Instruction 36–2406*. https://www.mcmilitarylaw.com/documents/afi_36-2406.pdf.

US Census Bureau. n.d. "U.S. Census Bureau QuickFacts: Emmett County, Michigan." https://www.census.gov/quickfacts/emmetcountymichigan.

US Department of Veterans Affairs. 2014. "Characteristics of Student-Veterans." *VA Campus Toolkit Handout*. https://www.mentalhealth.va.gov/studentveteran/docs/ed_todaysStudentVets.html.

US Department of Veterans Affairs. 2018. "How Common Is PTSD in Veterans?" https://www.ptsd.va.gov/understand/common/common_veterans.asp.

US Marines Corps. 2011. *USMC Fitness Report*. New York State Division of Military and Naval Affairs. https://dmna.ny.gov/forms/naval/NAVMC_10835__EF__5334.pdf.

US Marine Corps. n.d. Basic Officer Course. *Fitness Reports B3K3738 Student Handout*.

Instructor Guide for U.S. Navy Pride and Professionalism Workshop. 2008. General Dynamics Information Technology.

Vaccaro, Annemarie. 2015. "'It's Not One Size Fits All': Diversity *among* Student Veterans." *Journal of Student Affairs Research and Practice* 52 (4): 347–358.

Valentine, Kathryn. 2009. "'Acting Out' or Acts of Agency: WPA and 'Identities of Participation.'" In *The Writing Program Interrupted: Making Space for Critical Discourse*, edited by Donna Strickland and Jeanne Gunner, 147–154. Portsmouth, NH: Boynton/Cook.

Valentino, Marilyn J. 2012. "Serving Those Who Have Served: Preparing for Student-Veterans in Our Writing Programs, Classes and Writing Centers." *WPA* 36 (1): 164–178.

Villanueva, Victor. 2017. "Excerpt from *Bootstraps: From an American Academic of Color*." In *Writing about Writing: A College Reader*, edited by Elizabeth Wardle and Doug Downs, 116–127. Boston: Bedford/St. Martin's.

Wardle, Elizabeth. 2009. "'Mutt Genres' and the Goal of FYC: Can We Help Students Write the Genres of the University?" *College Composition and Communication* 60 (4): 765–789.

Weng, Fumei, France Cheong, and Christopher Cheong. 2010. "IT Education in Taiwan: Relationship between Self-Efficacy and Academic Integration among Students." *Innovations in Teaching & Learning in Information & Computer Sciences* 9 (2): 97–108.

Wheeler, Holly A. 2012. "Veterans' Transitions to Community College: A Case Study." *Community College Journal of Research and Practice* 36 (10): 775–792.

Wyatt, Linda G. 2011. "Nontraditional Student Engagement: Increasing Adult Student Success and Retention." *Journal of Continuing Higher Education* 59:10–20.

X, Malcolm. 2017. "Learning to Read." In *Writing about Writing: A College Reader*, edited by Elizabeth Wardle and Doug Downs, 106–114. Boston: Bedford/St. Martin's.

Yancey, Kathleen Blake, Liane Robertson, and Kara Taczak. 2014. *Writing across Contexts: Transfer, Composition, and Sites of Writing*. Logan: Utah State University Press.

Yin, Robert K. 2009. *Case Study Research: Design and Methods*. 4th ed. Thousand Oaks, CA: Sage.

Zacharakis, Jeffrey, and Jay A. Van Der Werff. 2012. "The Future of Adult Education in the Military." *New Directions for Adult and Continuing Education* 136:89–98.

Zajacova, Anna, Scott M. Lynch, and Thomas J. Espenshade. 2005. "Self-Efficacy, Stress, and Academic Success in College." *Research in Higher Education* 46 (6): 677–706.

ABOUT THE AUTHOR

Mark Blaauw-Hara is an assistant professor, teaching stream, at the University of Toronto–Mississauga. He has served as president of the Council of Writing Program Administrators, and his writing has appeared in *Composition Forum, Composition Studies, Kairos, Teaching English in the Two-Year College, The Journal of Teaching Writing,* and *The Community College Journal of Research and Practice,* among other journals. He has also written for several edited collections, including *(Re)Considering What We Know* (Adler-Kassner and Wardle) and *WPAs in Transition* (Wooten, Babb, and Ray), and he has been anthologized in collections such as *Teaching Composition at the Two-Year College* (Sullivan and Toth). Additionally, he serves on the editorial board of the *Journal of Veterans Studies.*

INDEX

Côté, James, 87
counseling centers, 33
counseling reports, army, 19, 27, 56–57, 66–68, 82, 83, 106
creativity, 80
"Crisis of Identity? Veteran, Civilian, Student" (ASHE), 86, 88, 98, 101–2
critical thinking, 24, 26
cuing for transfer, 105
culture, community, 78
culture shock, 33
curricula, clear objectives in, 38–39

data analysis, 13–17; focused coding, 13–14
decision making, and stress, 104
depression, 33, 102
Derek, 12, 14, 43; on military service, 25, 26; on peer support, 47–48
Developmental Counseling Form (US Army), 66–68
developmental courses, 103
disabilities, service-related, 102
discipline, 43, 44, 48
discourse requirements/rules, 93
diversity, 81; openness to, 44–45
Doe, Sue, *Generation Vet*, 6
Duckworth, Angela, on grit, 3–4

educational history, of adult learners, 86
emergence, of student identity, 87
emotions, 32, 107. *See also* anxiety; depression
error, in academic writing, 71
essays, 93
"An Ethical Obligation": Promising Practices for Student-Veterans in College Writing Classrooms, (Hart and Thompson), 6
Evaluation Report and Comprehensive Record, 64–65
evaluations, 19, 22, 59, 82–83; air force, 62–64; army, 66–68; marine corps, 60–62; navy, 64–65; writing, 56–57, 97; styles of, 68–69
expectations: clarifying, 50–51; standardization, 51–52
experience(s), 75; of adult learners, 91–92; life, 50, 90; military, 15–16, 96; prior, 24, 106–7; as threshold concept, 79–81, 84, 97; valuing, 45–46, 103, 104–5; veterans', 52–53; world, 44–45

faculty, 52, 104; academic membership and, 100–101; on academic writing, 69–72; knowledge of military writing, 55–56; survey of, 113–14

family, military as, 25
fear of brain rot, 33
feedback, 94
filtering, 70
first-year writing courses, 86, 101
Fitness Report (FitRep), 59, 60–62
flexibility, 104
format, military writing, 83
freedom, 104

Gee, James, 94
gender, 17
Generation Vet: Composition, Student-Veterans, and the Post-9/11 University (Doe and Langstraat), 6
genre analysis, 93
genres, 72, 81, 103; in military writing, 82–83, 95
GI benefits, 3
goals, 30, 43, 90, 91
Goffman, Erving, *Stigma*, 87
grading rubric, on evaluation forms, 64
grammar, 71
grit, 3–4, 6
grounded theory, constructivist, 9–10
group work, social setting of, 35
guidelines, 19

Hadlock, Erin, 58
Hart, Alexis, *"An Ethical Obligation,"* 6
higher-order thinking, 26
high-road transfer, 92–93, 105
Hinton, Corrine, on writing experiences, 80–81
Holton, Elwood, 103
hooks, bell, 92
human-centered methodology, 11

identity, identities, 16, 21, 75, 98; civilian, 101–2; community, 25–26, 100; learning shock and, 35–38; military, 25, 58–59, 96; performance of, 37–38, 84, 85–92; of student-veterans, 86–87; as threshold concept, 76–79, 97; transfer theory and, 105–6
individuality, college focus on, 90
initiative, 41
instruction manuals, 51, 52, 65
integration, social, 49–50, 54
interviews, 13, 15; coding, 14(table); participants, 11–12; student-veteran questions, 110–11
"Inventing the University" (Bartholomae), 85
isolation, social, 49
Ivanič, Roz, 37, 88; *Writing and Identity*, 10